W9-CES-716

WIN-WIN

WIN·WIN

APPROACHES TO CONFLICT RESOLUTION

ARNOLD GERSTEIN AND JAMES REAGAN

Foreword by
BRYANT WEDGE

Preface by
JAMES FOREST

✈P

GIBBS M. SMITH, INC.
PEREGRINE SMITH BOOKS
SALT LAKE CITY

EMERSON COLLEGE LIBRARY

HM
136
.G46
1986

This is a Peregrine Smith Book

Copyright © 1986 by Gibbs M. Smith, Inc.

No part of this book may be reproduced without
written permission from the publisher, with the
exception of short passages for review purposes

Published by Gibbs M. Smith, Inc. P.O. Box 667,
Layton, Utah 84041

Book design by J. Scott Knudsen
Printed in the United States of America

90 89 88 87 86   1 2 3 4 5

FIRST EDITION

**Library of Congress Cataloging-in-
Publication Data**

Gerstein, Arnold, 1940–
Win-win approaches to conflict resolution

Bibliography: p.
1. Social conflict.   2. Conflict management.
3. Interpersonal conflict.   I. Reagan, James, 1931–
II. Title.
HM136.G46   1986   303.6   85-26261
ISBN 0-87905-215-5

If only it were all so simple!
If only there were evil people somewhere
*   insidiously committing evil deeds,*
*   and it were necessary only to separate them*
*   from the rest of us and destroy them.*
But the line dividing good and evil
*   cuts through the heart of every human being.*
*   And who is willing to destroy*
*   a piece of his own heart?*

Aleksandr Solzhenitsyn
The Gulag Archipelago

CONTENTS

FOREWORD

The wonderful fact about win-win strategies is that everybody is expected, in the highest sense, to be true to his or her self. This is a book about making peace, but it is new in tone; there is no call for sacrifice here, nor for altruism, but a steady insistence on realism in the pursuit of one's interests.

In pursuing win-win strategies, the participants in conflict seek their advantage. What is new is the realization that this can often be gained without the discomfiture of competitors. Solutions that satisfy one's competitor's needs as well as one's own tend to be lasting. Win-lose strategies create enduring enemies for the winner and, sooner or later, the conflict cycle is apt to be resumed, sometimes at great cost to the original "winner." The realist looks for ways to connect pieces that solve problems which underlie disputes, while at the same time pursuing his or her own purposes.

The broad purpose of this volume is to introduce and illustrate a framework that looks to solutions that are maximally satisfying and minimally damaging to each of the parties. The realization that this is often possible is a new way of thinking; perhaps the new way that Albert Einstein called for to cope with the consequences of the unleashing of the atom. It will take time to sink in as minds change slowly, but Gerstein and Reagan provide a splendid launching pad. Those who read it are likely to benefit personally in the management of their own affairs, for there are many suggestions which are as applicable to business or marriage as to world-level disputes.

An immediate consequence of this realization is a striking shift in attitudes toward conflict. Most people and collectives have been taught to fear conflicts and hence to suppress them or avoid them, sometimes with quite Byzantine stratagems. This is because of the tendency of win-lose approaches to escalate toward violence or open warfare. Conflict is a dangerous event. When the possibility of managing conflicts in creative ways is discovered, their occurrence is less frightening and sometimes even welcomed. Conflicts become opportunities for exploring and solving all kinds of problems and inequities.

This attitude, too, is faithfully reflected in *Win-Win Approaches to Conflict Resolution,* where the beginning of the second chapter is a classic statement of the changed attitude. Conflict is not the problem — war is. As soon as it becomes evident that most conflicts need not lead to violence and that many disputes serve healthy purposes, it becomes possible to enter joyously into many contests; paradoxically the world (including personal worlds) may become noisier and safer at the same time. That is the experience of many conflict resolvers; people who have learned to quarrel productively become less prone to violent outbursts and destructive severings. The concept of disputatious peace is unfamiliar at first but soon becomes a lively practice for those who learn it.

I have said that these ideas are new, at least in a systematic sense. Game theory, from which the title is taken, is less than fifty years old. But that does not mean that they are marginal ideas. The term "conflict resolution" has already appeared in the language of presidents and chief justices. In October of 1984, the United States Congress established a United States Institute of Peace which incorporates the term and concepts of this emerging approach; over several years of debate we have seen senators and representatives grasp the central ideas and make them their own. This is extraordinarily rapid in the history of ideas and speaks for the basic authenticity of the approach.

The value of this work is that it presents something new in the management of our relationships to each other and to the world in a way that makes sense and appeals to our understanding of human behavior without asking for any basic change in the nature of man. I predict that within a decade the subject matter will be included in grade school curricula. By the end of this century several hundred thousand professionals will be serving as facilitators in conflict resolution. Law enforcers, military officers and diplomats will be familiar with the approach and will use it.

If, as I believe, this represents an idea whose time has come, it is timely indeed to be provided with an introduction that is both sophisticated and personal in its tone. It helps one to hope.

Bryant Wedge, M.D.
Washington, D.C.

PREFACE

Many of us live in a blaming society. We are aware of all sorts of things that are wrong and we can readily list people, groups, states, and philosophies that can be blamed. The list of those responsible for our troubles may well include the people we live with, neighbors, educators, politicians, church leaders, believers, non-believers, and maybe even dogs that aren't kept on a leash in the local park. We may well be the ones others are blaming for their troubles — our own children, for example, who blame us for what we did or didn't do in raising them; and we may blame them in return for their inability to understand or forgive. There are legions of lawyers who make their living by taking our blames to court and trying to turn them into cash which, even when obtained, may provide very chilly comfort.

Arnold Gerstein and James Reagan have dedicated their lives to finding a path from a grudge-collecting, blaming culture to one that is solution- and community-seeking. Perhaps the ideas the book contains will seem to you hopelessly and absurdly idealistic. Gerstein and Reagan openly consider ideals as necessary in determining historic direction, just as sailors consider a compass essential in finding their way under a cloudy sky. Such idealism is actually realism. What presently passes for realism has only made self-destruction more likely.

They are committed listeners, and in fact their book is mainly a guide to effective, creative listening—a deep listening that involves openness and vulnerability. In their stress on giving wholehearted attention to others, even those whom we feel threatened by, they remind me of a particular Buddhist saint—a *bodhisattva*—whose special gift was to pay such reverent, caring attention to each person he encountered that the other person became aware that he or she was the Buddha—already, in one sense, and in potentiality. This *bodhisattva* was a midwife for a second birth in life, able to help others give birth to a new self that had always been there but was hidden within layers of armor—that is, our layers of fear.

One of the nice things about the authors' teaching method is their stress on stories, some of which dramatize what good listening is all about. One of these, in the book's early pages, recalls a group of development experts who arrived in a Latin American village. They asked the villagers what it was they most needed. A statue of the Virgin Mary, the villagers replied. So the experts helped them get the statue. It was an unusual group of experts, for they didn't wait until they heard what they wanted to hear, but heard what was actually said. In this sense, the story is about a miracle. Experts are not famous for listening. (Perhaps the villagers, who were expert believers, made it possible for the development experts to discover a place for the Virgin Mary in their own hearts.)

Listening that is rooted in care for others, even strangers from very different cultural backgrounds, can have astonishing consequences. We discover that those strangers we have regarded as enemies have much in common with ourselves and that, if we can only begin to think together about problem solving, we can become allies and even partners in matters of immense importance. Change is possible — change in ourselves, change in others. We aren't trapped in the bad choices others have made, or that we ourselves have made.

For readers with any kind of religious faith, the authors offer affirmations of some of the more important, though often neglected, teachings in our faith traditions. We find that compassionate response to an enemy is not only an action of religious obedience but makes a great deal of sense. Such actions open the way to eliminate enmity. They help make possible the survival of our children (or the children of others) which violence and vengeance only threaten.

The authors lay great stress on both grief and forgiveness. In part this book is about the possibility of being released from those burdens which unforgiveness imposes on us. "Not forgiving is very hard on the stomach," a friend from Thailand recently pointed out to me. It is also hard on the soul. Our blaming society is so crippled by fear and anger that the life it offers is very grim fare. It can hardly be called life.

Whether talking about listening or forgiving, the authors are equipping us for active nonviolence: a way of life and social change that has developed in remarkable ways during this century, although, as Gandhi said, it is something as old as the hills. Active nonviolence is not simply a refusal to kill or harm others, but the daily seeking of restoration for damaged or broken relationships which are at the root of injustice and violence. It is a way of struggle that respects the humanity of adversaries and which consciously seeks reconciliation. But this isn't a painless way, as the authors remind us repeatedly. I am reminded of a passage from the writings of Thomas Merton: "As long as we are on earth, the love that unites us will bring us suffering by our very contact with one another, because this love is the resetting of a Body of broken bones."

This small book is refreshing to read. One of the things that makes it so hope giving is that it is so very practical and down-to-earth. The authors work from an extensive base of experience in situations others might easily consider impossible. They remind me of St. Catherine of Siena, a most practical mystic who was deeply involved in the creative resolution of conflict in her own time. She used to say, "All the way to heaven is heaven." I expect Arnie Gerstein and Jim Reagan would agree, for their whole approach is the connection of means and ends. Where we are going can be seen in the way we are getting there. The destination is in us as we move toward it.

Jim Forest
International Fellowship of Reconciliation
Alkmaar, Holland

ACKNOWLEDGMENTS

This book would not have been written without the wonderful and generous contributions from many individuals and organizations here and abroad. We are especially grateful to the following individuals who offered very valuable editorial assistance in the early stages of writing: Mary Weeks, Dick Joyce, and Jack Cirie. We also wish to express our appreciation to James Thomas of Gibbs M. Smith, Inc. for his diligent editing and continuous support.

INTRODUCTION

This started out as a polite book: Chicken Little was wrong, the sky is not falling. Despite all the conflict there is hope for peace and a better world. In the last year and a half, traveling around the world and lecturing, over and over again the two most common questions people ask are "Is there any hope?" and "Would anything we do make a difference?" Frankly, we are very concerned.

The sky may not be falling but it has a lot of cracks in it. While we wish to offer some hope and encouragement we do not see the tasks of resolving conflict to be simple or easy. We believe this book will be helpful, but it is not a "quick fix" or a panacea.

It is our intent to shed some light on the nature of human conflict and unmask what we feel are some myths and illusions that contribute to the difficulty of resolving conflict. It *is* possible to eliminate world hunger. This will significantly reduce the level of conflict and at the same time alleviate much of the unnecessary suffering and injustice in the world today. Another purpose is to present concrete tools people can use to resolve conflict in their personal lives.

The illusions of self-sacrifice, the glorification of dying as a way to rectify injustice, and compromising one's values are all archaic concepts. Rarely are human beings confronted with the lifeboat situation (four people have water for three and argue over who will live and who will die). Even in this example, there is a precedent for creative solutions in extreme situations.

We are disturbed by the dangerous collusive actions of world leaders who try to manage conflict by avoiding it. The illusory nature of their solutions is very transparent. We do not like solutions that relegate old men to skid row because they are no longer useful to the wheels of production. We are very concerned when corporations pursue economic solutions that exploit their employees and consumers to gain short-term profits for irresponsible stockholders. It is not enough, however, to be simply disturbed or concerned. These feelings emerge when one has lost certain illusions and ceases to collude in destructive activities. When these strong feelings are released they can be mobilizing, yet they do not determine our action.

We are all victims of our past illusions, the myths that we invented in the dark to protect us against what we did not understand.

France, Czechoslovakia, Switzerland, Sweden, the United States, and the Soviet Union, and who else we do not know, send weapons of destruction indiscriminately around the world to third world countries struggling to learn the rudiments of self-government, while the amount of aid for education, health, welfare, and agriculture is negligible.

We have no quarrel with the mother tiger who defends her young or the black widow who is guarding her eggs outside our window box this summer. We do not see her polluting her web, devising plans to disrupt the entire structure of the planet. We believe that humans are as capable as cats and dogs, tigers and spiders, of coming up with solutions to insure a life for future generations. We are not interested in being participants in the end to history for the human race.

This book is for those of you who still have the energy to participate in a different sort of game, one that has to do with living, and with solving conflicts for all mankind, not just some special interest group which claims to have "the right answer," or a special claim to "divine wisdom."

Lectures by bureaucrats in the State Department about the stupidity of Jews, Arabs, Latin Americans and Egyptians are tiring. Revolutionary rhetoric that implies the only solution is to "kill the enemy" is archaic. We are tired of lectures about original sin and the lack of man's perfectibility. We are also tired of the press and television news people who report only the disasters, rapes, murders, political blunders of politicians, and rarely give two minutes' time to the people we have met in our travels who are still working, however clumsily, to make this planet livable.

We have had army officers plead with us to come up with better alternatives to defend the country they love than the nuclear physicists have offered. We would like to enlist those of you who are still in touch with pain and injustice, those of you who care, who can still mobilize enough passion to go to work with all your strength and will, to tackle the tough problems our complex world presents to us. We are practical idealists. It is in this spirit we offer both a conceptual framework as well as concrete tools people can use to resolve conflict.

PART ONE

THE NATURE OF CONFLICT

CHAPTER ONE

Conflict and the Larger Process

Our purpose in approaching conflict as a natural part of a larger life process is to provide a context that can open up more options and alternatives for bringing about resolutions that benefit as many people in any conflict situation as possible. The operating assumption that "one is right from one's own perspective" is not a conciliatory strategy; it helps shift the entire focus from defending positions to a firm and strong search for a blending of interests and needs. This provides a framework in which to develop a network of responsibility and caring so that win-win outcomes are possible.

It is possible to learn not to be choked by discord, instability and imbalance. Only by experiencing imbalance are we able to experience a state of balance. By learning how to be more attentive to developmental change we can anticipate and intelligently cope with conflict. The resolution of conflict facilitates a higher level of social organization that can meet more people's needs.

There is a need to plan ahead for conflict so that violent forceful solutions are not needed. Human beings have the capacity to be responsive and resources are available to meet all their needs. It is extremely important to respect the integrity of the individual and the interdependency of all people on this planet. To do this we must take back the power we have given away to the experts and enter into a partnership with people who have certain technical expertise or specialized areas of knowledge. This entails giving up our belief of helplessness and our positions as victims. Win-win is possible when people work together with intention and sincerity.

Conflict is a natural occurrence that is part of a larger process of growth, development, and change. This is not to say that the behaviors of people in conflict, and the solutions invented by those people, are part of some natural unfolding of the universe. They are not. Human beings are creative and inventive, as is nature, but many of these creations and inventions simply don't work. They need to be discarded. The approach presented here will enable people, if they are genuinely committed, to find ways of navigating through conflict and to develop new possibilities for living in the world.

We are less concerned with improving the world and eliminating conflict than enabling people to respond constructively in conflict situations. A major characteristic of conflict situations has to do with events and people being seriously out of balance with their environment, and there is often nothing at all wrong with this state of being except that some of the solutions people use when they are out of balance don't work.

For example, let's consider a child going from crawling and scooting to walking upright. In moments of frustration he may attack the floor or attempt to defy the laws of gravity. He may have dreams of magically removing all the furniture in the room to make walking easier. Yet over time it is the latent capacities of the child that win out. Once he has learned to navigate upright he no longer fantasizes about changing the world in the same ways. There is no need to curse the ground or the furniture in the room which only seemed to be in his way. The child has gone from a crawling stage (which is a balance state) to a new and steadier state of equilibrium. Ineffectual responses to conflict situations occur as well during later stages of growth. We habitually become irritated and frustrated when our interaction with the environment does not work (conflict). We blame or curse the food, the stove, the cook, the car, and ourselves, in fact anyone who unfortunately happens to be nearby. We may even blame nature and God in order to avoid the responsibility of seeking solutions that work and are harmonious and thereby move beyond our dependency on responses that do not. Development and change challenge the status quo because old forms are destroyed and new forms emerge. Stress and crisis, dissent and chaos, the stuff of conflict, is natural and necessary if opportunity is to emerge.

As society becomes more complex, the challenge is to create order out of increasing instability. The mind naturally seeks meaning and moves to organize the disorder and see new patterns of connection. A moment of understanding, learning something new, falling in love, or any other "shock wave" event reshuffles the elements of the whole.

"Evolution is a continuous breaking and forming to make new, richer wholes," according to Ferguson in *The Aquarian Conspiracy*. Crisis and conflict alert us to the fact that solutions we have designed to deal with previous situations may no longer work.

The natural process of which conflict is a part can best be illustrated by the chart on the following page.

Our lives seem to swing from those idyllic, precious moments when we are in some marvelous state of balance (I on chart), to various states of imbalance: from pinprick irritations to the desire for novelty, a new toy, a larger view out of our crib. Even our dogs and cats experience this shift from placid contentment to wanting to see what is going on in the next room. A world of development and new orientation is being entered (II on chart). We know this pattern well, yet it always catches us by surprise. For years, a cat has spent every afternoon in the same chair where the sun shines in through the window. One day, for no apparent reason, she decides to move one of the dogs

PROCESS MODEL OF CONFLICT

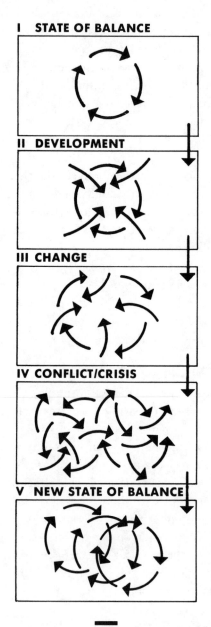

from his place on the rug. In the next three weeks every animal in the house (all six) begin a search for a new order (III on chart). There are many fights, disagreements, and an occasional, noisy discussion (IV on chart). Then all is calm again — only each animal has a new place (V on chart).

The social and political adjustments made in the world since World War II provide an example of "repositioning" on a human, and much grander scale. The industrial nations undertook the most complex and extensive interaction with the non-industrial nations of the world. This development did not begin in 1945, but its global visibility was vastly accelerated. With this development has come inevitable change. Like so many sleeping dogs and cats, people are waking up all over the world. The noise level increases. To those of us asleep this seems an enormous inconvenience, and to those of us awake it means an increase in the level of excitement and conflict.

Both of these examples view conflict in a developmental frame of reference. How one looks at conflict determines one's actions in a conflict situation. When the conflict situation itself is seen as an irritant, one may want to change the situation quickly or run to avoid it through improvement programs based on some romantic view of the past or a utopian future. At a more extreme level, one might seek to eliminate the situation or persons one is in conflict with because of the feeling of danger or threat. We believe a better solution is to try to find ways for a new dynamic balance of all the elements within the conflict situation, and our approach to conflict resolution is based on the following assumptions.

OPERATING ASSUMPTIONS FOR APPROACHING CONFLICT

1. **All needs are legitimate.**
2. **There are enough resources to meet all the needs.**
3. **Within every individual lies untapped power and capacity.**
4. **Process is as important as content.**
5. **Improving situations is different from solving problems.**
6. **Everyone is right from his or her own perspective.**
7. **Solutions and resolutions are temporary states of balance.**

1. All needs are legitimate.

All needs are considered important and must be attended to. When we use the term "need" we are referring to basic needs that maintain human beings and ensure growth and development. Often when people use the word "need" they are actually presenting solutions to meet a basic need and not addressing the need itself, as when someone says "he *needs* to go to a concert." Going to a concert is a solution to a need such as "hearing music" or "the need for social contact," and only one of many possible solutions to those needs. When all needs are considered of equal importance the task shifts to a search for options to meet all the needs. This is different from seeing the task as having to prove which need should be addressed. In working with conflict situations, such as strife in the home, we find that people come together and argue over different needs. A wife may focus on the need for growth while the husband concentrates on security needs, so that it is exceedingly difficult for either side to hear the needs of the other.

For convenience we have outlined three broad categories of needs: *Growth needs* include the need for feelings of self-esteem, love, inclusion, curiosity, and the need for opportunities to learn new information and acquire new skills. *Security needs* include the need for feelings of safety and protection, and the need for the basics of survival, food, water, and shelter. A third important category is the *need to manage pain and injury*. Virtually all of us have suffered pain, injury, and loss. If the need to express anger, pain, and grief is not acknowledged, other means are found to manage pain: chronic arguing, subtle and not so subtle forms of retribution, and revenge. Also, when pain and injury are not addressed they can lead to depression, and even to violent outbursts that can end in murder or suicide.

2. There are enough resources to meet all the needs.

Synergy is a highly complex concept which includes the idea that new sources of energy in the form of ideas, institutions, or tools emerge from an integration of parts. The concept of synergy tells us that we can do more with less, and that the whole is richer than its parts. Synergy also implies the importance of human beings as central to any synergistic process. Our traditional belief that there is a limited amount of resources available is often a function of leaving human creativity out of our accounting systems. The systems then only measure material wealth. Yet it has been the exercise of human creativity that has accounted for the tools and techniques that have reduced effort and energy in order to produce more and to improve the quality of life.

It is common to only see wealth in material terms. For example, if you have ten TV sets you could say you have ten units of wealth. At this level of analysis what is not being counted is the information being broadcast and communicated through the sets. This has broad implications for world poverty and infant mortality rates in developing countries. One key factor in reducing the infant mortality rate in Bahrain from 120 to 34 per thousand in one year was a television campaign educating people in child care and breast-feeding. The missing resource contributing to the crisis situation was lack of appropriate information, not lack of food or material resources.

Yet another level of synergy can be seen working on the psycho-social level. There is more human love radiating the less we hold in and bind up our energy through game playing, competition, possessiveness, and jealousy. The more we give out selflessly, the more comes back to us. The same holds true for information. When it is given freely we still have it with us, and as it is shared there is greater wealth for all of us. In fact all of us collectively know more than any one of us. Brainstorming in a group reveals the exponential power of this synergistic process. The group comes alive through cooperative action; and information and creativity abound because of the non-judgmental climate, the relaxation of competition and the opening of positive feelings.

Our traditional conception of intelligence is of an isolated operation within our heads. More recent views maintain that this is too narrow a conception. One needs to also think of intelligence as the collective interaction between people as they are engaged in cooperative tasks. Recent experiments in group problem solving have shown almost a tenfold increase in efficiency and output over individuals working in isolation. Isolation and competition hinder output because each member of the group is not benefiting from the development of every other member.

Synergy can also be witnessed at the level of breakthrough technology. Recently a small group of inventors using simple tools like a screwdriver, a wrench, a saw, and very common materials put together a complex tool which uses solar energy to pump water. Here we have an interaction between the minds of the inventors who produced the design, simple tools, raw materials, and human labor. In combination they bring about an increase in real wealth that is greater than the wealth of each part by itself. Furthermore, there was a great savings in terms of future labor, in non-renewable energy, and in basic material costs, not to mention that a pump of this kind is needed throughout the developing world where in 1983, according to the World Bank, 2.5 billion people lacked adequate water supplies.

Further evidence of the connection between synergy, wealth, and positive outcomes could be cited. The evidence can be seen when one studies the functioning of self-organization and self-government in cooperatives, bartering systems, mutual help networks, credit unions, and other structures where resources are pooled and there is a uniting of individual will and intention leading to outcomes that are mutually beneficial. This is what win-win is all about.

Resources will also be more abundant when we make distribution systems less dependent on persuading people to have what we think they should have. Finally, if solutions are designed to meet the needs they were designed to meet, we will save considerably on energy and resources. Solutions that destroy resources, like paying farmers not to produce or subsidizing industries that use obsolete equipment, will certainly erode wealth.

3. Within every individual lies untapped power and capacity.

This may seem like an obvious statement, yet in many educated circles there is deception and pessimism about people's ability to take care of themselves and each other. While many of the world's people lack information and tools to better their lives, they usually exhibit a determination and creativity in the use of what they do have. This innate wisdom is often unseen by educated westerners who have not been taught to look for it. It is also the authors' experience that people in conflict know better what they need than outside experts.

Years ago one of the authors got a call from a school social worker who informed him that one of his clients, a six-year-old girl, had a serious sexual problem which needed immediate attention. The little girl was touching her genitals in class. When she went into the counseling clinic she was asked why she was doing that and she said, "I have a rash." She did. The teachers and social workers had not bothered to ask her why she was doing what she was doing. They explained her behavior with a theory about sexual neurosis.

People's ability to know what they need can also be seen in what recently occurred in an Indian village in South America. A development team went to the village where there was great poverty and asked the villagers what they wanted for their children. Unlike many development field workers who do not ask — much less consider — what people might want, this group did. The villagers said they wanted a statue of the Virgin Mary in the village square. The development team then offered to help them accomplish this task without questioning their need. The villagers became willing partners and learned about community organization and how to work cooperatively with some modern tools. After the statue was built, the team asked the villagers what they wanted next for their children. They responded by asking for a vegetable garden. This was quickly accomplished. Had the team tried to impose their own "solution" based on their idea of the villagers' problem, i.e., inadequate food production, these proud people would have thrown them out and rightly so. Moreover, they would have sacrificed their self-respect and integrity in order to build a garden imposed by outsiders and have soon lost the trust and respect of their children. When a parent does not feel self-esteem and security within, the child no longer feels safe and secure and begins to lose trust in the parent.

4. Process is as important as content.

Process is extremely important in a conflict situation for it is the overall direction, and unfolding of events. Process is also what is moving into focus in a specific interaction. It is the flow of feelings, thoughts, and events. If one becomes too fixed on particular details of content one loses important valuable clues and information about what is going on and what people are doing.

In our work with individuals or groups in conflict, we have frequently observed that there is relatively little watching and listening taking place. Yet these are the main tools for understanding the process. Often the intended listener is so caught up in specific pieces of content, either rehearsing an attack or thinking of evidence to support a position, that the process going on is totally missed.

In the fall of 1983 at Esalen, a center for the study of human growth and potential, a group of military officers from the Monterey Post Graduate School were brought together with some Soviet emigres to engage in simulation games. This project was designed to explore ways to more effectively deal with Soviet-American relationships. One afternoon a two-hour dialogue took place between the two groups, the Americans and the Russians. The Americans continually made suggestions about how to improve various situations and the Russians expertly found flaws in all the solutions offered. At the end the Americans felt frustrated with the Russians' "negativism," and the Russians felt frustrated by the Americans' "lack of sophistication." What neither group observed was the process itself, a very predictable dance with a predictable outcome — the Americans offering solutions and the Russians rejecting them. This process could have been modified or changed had it been observed by the participants. The Americans might have stopped offering solutions and asked the Russians for some. Or the Russians could have initiated some solutions of their own.

5. Improving situations is different from solving problems.

Resolutions that are aimed at improving a situation are better than solutions that attempt to eliminate specific problems. When we focus on conflict we often attempt to eliminate the problem and rarely address the underlying causes. In America we have tried to eliminate feelings of stress through running and aerobics. Physical tension as well as emotional tension is indeed reduced by exercising in this way. However, the underlying causes of stress-related tension, such as the way we work with others and resolve conflicts, is usually overlooked. We are more excited about getting rid of the tension (i.e., "the problem") than in improving the stressful situation, and once again we become distracted by partial solutions.

Similarly, the debate between pro-life groups and the advocates of abortion rarely centers on the broader question of sexual-social education of boys and girls, and the cultural support systems that would maximize the growth and development of men and women. Appropriate child care and child rearing and the role of men and women are underlying issues that are ignored. Extreme emotional investment in solutions inhibits the exploration of broader ramifications. During sessions given on conflict resolution recently in California, we discovered that the pro-abortion people had been invited by pro-life people to enter into dialogue, and the pro-abortion people rejected the invitation. Had they been able to enter into dialogue it is our belief that they would have discovered that their common needs and interests were greater than their differences. Many of the partial solutions to specific problems are no longer in conflict when recombined into a more encompassing approach. This increases the possibility of addressing more areas of concern and a larger number of human needs.

In Egypt there is a high infant mortality rate and a high birthrate. Egypt adds one million people to her population every ten months; this places the country in a race against time for agricultural development. The Egyptians are quick to point out that birth control and family planning do not take into account:

1. Problems of economic development.
2. The importance of children as a social institution for the care of the elderly.
3. The religious and cultural values of the Egyptian people.

6. Everyone is right from his or her own perspective.

One way to avoid intensifying conflict is to acknowledge the essential validity of another person's reality or point of view. Once this is done we may be able to enter into it and see what it is composed of. In aikido, a martial art used to reconcile conflict, this is known as *irimi*. We move forward toward the attack to find the opening. In denying aggression or in fighting back we only intensify the conflict with two kinds of messages to the attacker: (1) "don't be aggressive," "turn the other cheek," "keep your hands in your pocket," or (2) "get out of my way," "I'll get back at you." In aikido we enter into the place of attack but at the last instant we can pivot, change our body position, or walk away. We are at the place where the attack came from, and now we are standing next to the other person, able to see the origin of the attack, but without getting hurt or needing to hurt the attacker. It is possible that if we move inside the situation to see it from the attacker's perspective we can come up with a resolution more favorable to both of us.

This can be illustrated by an imaginary dialogue that describes position and point of view. Imagine that you are facing me in a room. We each see the wall behind the other person. Where each of us is standing is our position. I say, "In my reality I see you and a wall with a window and a picture of a vase with flowers. Now that's reality." You disagree and say, "No, that's not reality, I see a wall with a door and a fireplace. There is no window and I am sure there is no picture with a vase of flowers." We believe we are both right, and only by one or both of us leaving our position can we see what the other is talking about. In this simple example we both have an opportunity to enlarge our respective views of reality, or we can stick to our positions and deny the validity of the other person's reality. Let's say I want to climb out the window and you, who see the door, want to open it. If I am willing to move in order to see your point of view I, too, will see the door and have the choice of climbing out the window or leaving through the door. If you wanted the door open to let in some air and gave up your position, you would discover the window and also have a choice to either open the window or the door for more air.

In many conflict situations people spend an inordinate amount of time defending or supporting their positions and points of view. This can be an exhausting and wasteful diversion. Although from our example it would seem we are limiting "position" to a geographical place, we must add that a person's position is much more inclusive and contains all of their prior experiences and expectations as well as their current needs.

Continual arguing only teaches people newer ways to argue and leads to lose-lose outcomes. Practice makes perfect. What we recommend when people are engaged in defending their positions is very simple. We ask them to just stop for a moment and decide: do they really want to get their needs met, or would they rather go on arguing with themselves and with others. If they choose to go on arguing, we tell them that when they are finished arguing we will be available to help them find ways to optimize their needs.

7. Solutions and resolutions are temporary states of balance.

Resolutions and solutions are not absolute or timeless. They are dependent upon the flux of circumstances and human changeability. That is why most contracts are renegotiable and not irrevocable. The phrase "I changed my mind" is not necessarily a childish statement. The difference between an adult changing his mind and a child is that we expect an intelligent adult to let us know when he has done so. When circumstances change we also expect an adult to recognize those changes and alter his actions.

Since situations and people develop and fluctuate, any resolution arrived at must also be subject to reformulation so a dynamic balance can be reached.

CHAPTER TWO

The Character of Conflict

Over the years conflict has taken various forms within our imagination. Sometimes it appears as an avenging angel sent by God to punish people. At other times dissension and conflict appear as a silver-tongued orator, who with barbed words destroys all our cherished beliefs and thoughts. In some families he is so feared that everyone agrees to ignore him and children are taught to only say nice things. "If you can't say something nice, be silent" (i.e., be agreeable). Conflict is forced underground where it remains a mysterious force that must be strenuously avoided.

There are cultures where verbal conflict is avoided at all costs. Being polite and lying become institutionalized. Driving conflict underground, however, usually only delays its arrival on the surface, and guarantees that when it appears it will appear in a more painful way. Meanwhile, those who carry the conflict feel off-center, torn, under attack, in turmoil and lonely, even unappreciated. Yet this is not always the case.

In some families and cultures conflict is seen as a clever child who is rewarded for disagreeing and arguing. Some groups encourage arguing, and the more visible conflict becomes the better everyone feels. It is as if they feel that "there's gotta be something wrong here so let's smoke it out now or maybe even create something wrong."

Conflict can even manifest itself as a noble cause, a woman in white who must be saved from the barbarian hordes while people cheer and wave the brave young men off to war. It is not uncommon to hear older men in America complain about our recent wars, that they were not good wars because the enemy was not clearly bad or evil. Sometimes conflict can appear as a complex web that people run from because they were taught life should be simple and painless and that complexity is beyond human understanding.

In western tradition conflict has long been associated with wars; yet there is nothing inherent in conflict to support this. Conflict does not cause war, although war is one solution to conflict; it is exceedingly hard, however, to separate the two in our minds. Historically, people have suffered so much pain and death from war and fighting that the mere mention of "conflict" arouses images of tension, death, and destruction. Consequently, conflict is often avoided and important change is swept aside until the needs reemerge at more dramatic levels, increasing the appeal to violent solutions.

Even the language describing conflict is permeated with military terminology: "Let's attack the problem," "Join the War on Poverty," "The International Peace Brigades," "Moral imperatives of defeating President Reagan," "It's important to fight it out," "The nomination battle." The name of a recent book on conflict resolution is entitled *Fighting to Win*. A headline in the *Rocky Mountain News* reads: "Hart: Battle now switches to Mondale vs. Reagan." Another book about male-female relationships is entitled *The Intimate Enemy*. And movements like The Gray Panthers, Women's Liberation Movement, and Gay Liberation place "conflict" in a fight or aggressive mode.

When we view conflict as a natural process, our minds are less cluttered by thoughts of avoidance and fear, aggression or anger. In this chapter we will look at this process in terms of what people bring to the conflict situation and how the various levels of conflict interact and impinge upon the conflict resolver.

WHAT PEOPLE BRING TO THE CONFLICT SITUATION

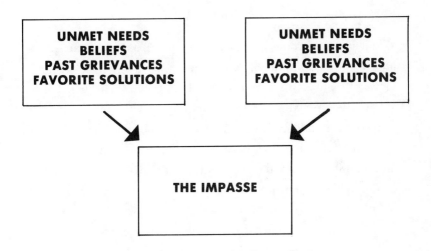

UNMET NEEDS
BELIEFS
PAST GRIEVANCES
FAVORITE SOLUTIONS

UNMET NEEDS
BELIEFS
PAST GRIEVANCES
FAVORITE SOLUTIONS

THE IMPASSE

The Impasse

The impasse is a focal point in any conflict situation. It's the place where people have come together to attempt some resolution of the current difficulties. It is also a period of time where everyone appears blocked from any avenue to a successful outcome. There are no solutions in sight that are satisfactory to all the people involved, and a stalemate results. What people bring to the impasse and struggle over are unmet needs, beliefs, past grievances, and favorite positions.

Unmet Needs

Needs are rarely talked about when people come into a conflict situation. Needs are very difficult to clarify at this point because they are so mixed up with people's favorite solutions and beliefs. The unstated needs give critical momentum in keeping people together until they resolve their difficulties.

Beliefs

When any two groups get together at the impasse they can spend an inordinate amount of time arguing about their beliefs and views of reality, and they can use the differences in their belief systems as the main obstacle to coming up with any options for resolving the conflict. Most professional negotiators are in agreement that struggling over positions and beliefs is non-productive, although it can help to clarify, early in the negotiating process, certain beliefs that people may have that can interfere with what they have really come to deal with.

On the following pages are two sets of beliefs. The negative ones keep us from acting for mutual gain, and they paralyze cooperative negotiating. The positive ones facilitate win-win resolutions.

BELIEFS THAT LEAD TO IMPASSES

1. "It is impossible to solve anything. Life and its difficulties are too complex and beyond the capacity of humankind to deal with."
2. "I feel helpless so let's argue."
3. "This is my territory/property. I own this."
4. "Stand fast, don't give up."
5. "Things don't work out."
6. "You can't expect too much."
7. "Someone has to suffer."
8. "There are a lot of things that are none of your/my business."
9. "Don't ask dumb questions."
10. "There is not enough time."
11. "This can't make a difference."
12. "This is just the way it is."
13. "You just can't get anywhere with certain people."
14. "Man is basically flawed."
15. "You have to compromise."
16. "There will always be winners and losers."
17. "You can't really trust anyone."

BELIEFS THAT LEAD TO
WIN-WIN RESOLUTIONS

1. "It is possible to solve problems. Life and its complexities are well within the capacity of humankind to deal with."
2. "I am powerful and adaptive and do not need to argue."
3. "This is our territory, our planet."
4. "Navigate and be willing to let go."
5. "Many things do work."
6. "Expect a lot of self and others."
7. "Much of human suffering can be eliminated and avoided."
8. "Everything is our business."
9. "There are no dumb questions."
10. "There is plenty of time. People only act in the present and it is always only NOW."
11. "It is impossible not to make a difference."
12. "This is just one of the ways it is."
13. "You can get somewhere with anyone."
14. "Humankind is basically endowed with all the equipment to survive and adapt in this world."
15. "Compromise is only one option among many for resolving conflict."
16. "It is possible for everyone to win."
17. "It is possible to learn to trust ourselves and others."

We are not questioning the truth or falsity of any of these beliefs; however, the negative ones all interfere with resolving conflicts within a win-win structure. They also discourage people from running risks and discovering new options.

We have found that keeping this list in mind is very helpful when dealing with people in conflict. Each of the negative beliefs, when it arises, is a sign that the process is about to break down. Our own style is to attend to these beliefs when they first arise.

Someone, for instance, is suggesting that something be tried and another person says, "There isn't enough time." We might agree and say, "You're right, there may not be enough time. So shall we quit?" Or, "What are we going to do with the time we have? Can you suggest something that would make it possible to do anything in the time we have?" The point is, we do not want to lose the person because of his or her belief even though it is leading to a crisis point. If the person's belief is pushed aside or argued with, most likely he or she will cease to be a part of a constructive team trying to improve things.

An important cause for long diversions into positional struggles is a belief that there are only limited resources available and we must compete for them because there are not enough to go around. This belief justifies the need for war, domination, and control. Somehow it is perfectly all right to make sacrifices of one's own people or others for the good of the whole. With these beliefs operating, the discussion gets focused on how much people are willing to give up or how much they are willing to lose.

Until recently, divorce negotiations and proceedings were based on lawyers instructing their clients in what to relinquish in order to gain something else. Mutual needs were rarely addressed. The results were mistrust, animosity, and arbitrary rulings. With the advent of divorce arbitration, conflict is now frequently resolved by the use of win-win methods to bring about mutual gain.

Pentagon arguments about *how many* cities we are willing to give up in defense of the United States, *how many* soldiers we are willing to sacrifice on the battlefield, and *how much* wealth we are willing to lose in order to protect our long-run interests, are plans for a win-lose scenario.

It is important to intervene if we are to move beyond the impasse to a deeper level where we can choose an alternative that is not self-defeating or negatively self-fulfilling. We may ask if both sides would be willing to set aside their belief systems for some alternatives such as those on the positive list with no guarantee they will work. In the process of working with these positive beliefs there is the possibility of discovering options and strategies that no one has yet thought of to make it possible for all needs to be met without any sacrifices. This, of course, involves running risks. The negative beliefs we have listed are risk-free.

People in dispute frequently believe it impossible for both sides to get their needs met. To stimulate the resolution process we agree that they may be right, that it may be impossible for there to be mutual gain on both sides. Nevertheless, we ask if they would be willing to gamble with us and spend some time exploring our belief that mutual gain is possible. The request, which can be made by anyone in a conflict situation, is usually met with interest and acceptance. Our experience in the United States and in the Middle East has been that people are tired of hostility and fighting over ideologies and positions and are beginning to consider that there are enough resources to go around. Both sides can win!

Past Grievances

In long-standing conflict situations people arrive at the impasse with grievances, some stated and others unstated. Many approaches to conflict resolution do not deal with these grievances. Grievances are avoided with the same intensity that people avoid conflict. They are swept aside by being labeled irrational or irrelevant, as if somehow the grievances are not legitimate issues in resolving conflict. Each side can tell the other, "You must forget about the past," "I don't want to hear past history," or "Let us go on from here."

Unfortunately, the past must be worked through and released. If you were to tell a married couple that they had to forget the past and disregard their grievances and unmet needs there would be an escalation of win-lose tactics. Holding onto grievances is as unproductive as trying to bury them unattended or discounted. People want to be treated as equals and attending to past grievances, "past history," is an important way to do that.

We have presented some of the traditional attitudes and beliefs about conflict that make it such a disagreeable subject. We are not suggesting that any of us are going to surrender all of our stereotyped attitudes or knee-jerk reactions when our attention is called to another conflict. Working intelligently and sensitively with conflict situations is difficult and time consuming. Great care must be taken not to get overtired and burned out; fatigue leads to thoughts of wishing to be somewhere else or trying to hurry up and get through it. Most of the discipline in conflict resolution work is in *listening, observing*, and *gathering* information; not in simply doing something! It is more important to know when to do something than what to do.

Years ago one of the authors got permission from his clinical staff to spend an extended period of time observing a sixteen-year-old boy who had been diagnosed as mentally retarded. The staff had recommended his placement in a home for the mentally retarded. The observation continued for six months, two hours weekly, in the office; we spoke very little. One day I asked if he heard voices. He nodded: "Yes." "What were the voices saying?" I asked. "To kill you," he replied. I suggested that the voices must be afraid of me. The boy agreed. I asked if his voices would be willing to talk to me and he said they would. For the next couple of months the boy's "voices" and I talked. The voices were not mentally retarded. He continued to see me and attended a group with other adolescents, learned to play, socialize, and began dating. This young man is now married and raising a family. Six months of observation seemed like a long time to me, but to this boy who had spent much of his thirteen years in hospitals and who faced a future in institutions for the mentally retarded, six months was negligible. Techniques and demands to hurry up and get things done will sometimes interfere with being effective and bringing about real and lasting resolutions.

It took over ten years of patient negotiating for the United States and Panama to work out a solution to the Panama Canal dispute that was acceptable to both sides. As in the previous example, what made the negotiations successful was the willingness of two of the key negotiators from each side to become personally involved with each other and develop, *over a number of years*, a genuine sense of trust and caring. They both took the time to become thoroughly acquainted with the concerns and needs of the other side.

Levels of Conflict

So far we have been looking at some of the specific elements of conflict. Let us now shift our focus and broaden our perspective of the conflict situation by looking at various levels of conflict.

In studying the following diagram it will be useful to keep in mind that conflict, as a natural process, has many levels. Like the parts of a living organism, the levels are all equally vital and interdependent. At any point on any level there are specific individual human beings making decisions.

We have often met with frustrated individuals who tell us that they can't solve a particular problem because of the system, the schools, the government, or the military establishment. Our response is that one does not negotiate or conduct encounters with organizations — only with people. An organization is an abstraction and abstractions don't make decisions, only people do. Feelings of helplessness and alienation grow from the entrapment in abstraction; for example "the political system," "town hall," or "the city." Power and flexibility are reborn when

LEVELS OF CONFLICT

Ecological Level—restraints of the environment, including climate, limits of fresh water, agricultural land, location of resources, i.e., oil, gas, minerals, lakes, rivers, mountains, plains.

Ecological Level—restraints of the environment, including climate, limits of fresh water, agricultural land, location of resources, i.e., oil, gas, minerals, lakes, rivers, mountains, plains.

INTERNATIONAL LEVEL
Super-Powers
Multi-National
Groups

REGIONAL LEVEL
i.e., Middle East, Latin America, Western Europe, Southeast Asian Countries, etc.

NATIONAL LEVEL

LOCAL LEVEL
Cities, State, Villages,
Local Interest Groups

FAMILY LEVEL
Clans, Tribes,
Religious Groups,
Language Groups

INDIVIDUAL LEVEL
at different life stages—male/female

one can think about "Mary, the city clerk," "Bufford, the manager," and "Col. Jones, the commander." The former is fantasy, the latter is personal, accessible, and true.

One needs to treat the diagram like a sailing chart which leaves out the waves, wind conditions, currents, boats, and fish. A diagram is useful in telling where we are but does not inform us about specific conditions.

When studying the diagram it is important to realize that any given person can be representing needs and interests on different levels, many of which are not fully conscious. This may account for hidden agendas, delay, and avoidance in the resolution process.

Two statesmen sitting across a bargaining table are struggling over an international conflict. They are individuals, very likely with families and grandchildren, are members of local communities, and are concerned about their personal or career goals. They have responsibilities at every level the diagram outlines. Details at all levels are working upon their minds and hearts, and affect everyone.

This is no less true in our own personal lives. How a housewife and husband feed their children affects the evolution of that child, his interaction with others, even future health and disease patterns. Moreover, their buying habits and the use of energy have far-reaching impact on the national and international economy and on the condition of the environment. Conflict is a process that is experienced and dealt with by humans with multiple agendas representing a number of interacting levels on the diagram.

Integrity and Cultural Values

The interplay of individual integrity, personal needs, and cultural values has a profound effect on conflict resolution at the international level. In the spring of 1945 meetings took place between King Abdul Aziz of Saudi Arabia and Franklin Delano Roosevelt, and between Abdul Aziz and Winston Churchill, on the issue of Palestine. Roosevelt was the first "infidel" head of state he (Abdul Aziz) had met in all his sixty-nine years. Roosevelt had utmost respect for the king's prohibition of alcohol and smoking and only smoked and drank in private. Churchill insisted on his right to smoke cigars and drink alcohol at any time during, before, and after meals in the king's presence. The king struggled with Churchill's highhanded ways and his "big stick" approach. The smoking and drinking may not have interfered as much had Churchill been more open to the king's view on Palestine. We are suggesting that a portion of the king's non-receptivity to Churchill was due to Churchill's individual style and manner. The king returned home on a British cruiser without being offered any of the amenities. There were no gunnery demonstrations, no tents on the deck, and there was no fraternizing with the crew. This lack of attention to the king's human needs and values became a long standing grievance which increased the difficulties in subsequent interactions between Saudi Arabia and Great Britain.

The Illusion of Power at the Top

It is a not-so-well-kept secret that in high level positions of authority we may actually have limited power and feel and act helpless and vulnerable. This is true in Washington and Rome as well as in Moscow and London. At the present time our federal government seems totally bogged down and incapable of getting any work done. It is the result of a radical shift in the way people are organizing their lives at a grass roots level. What has undermined government from the top is not only the spread of democratic ideas of people sold on the American way of life, it is the overall availability of every kind of information imaginable as well. In large part this availability is facilitated by the miniaturization of radios and cassettes. We have begun to reach the level of a global village.

The Kennedy mystique contributed to a more expanded distribution of power: "Ask not what your country can do for you, but what you can do for your country." Anyone, regardless of his station in life, can do something. A call to action and the recognition of individual power and self-reliance affects not only Americans but people all over the world. Everyone is involved in some form of self-determination, from urban neighborhoods in America to villagers in Africa and Indians in South America, and this involvement is calling forth a new view of leadership. Fewer passive followers are willing to take advice from the top. Leaders in Lebanon find that before they can even meet to set up a government they must first discover who will follow them.

To be effective at higher levels, decision makers need to take into consideration the increasing power of individuals at the lower levels who have access to more information than ever before. Followers need to give leaders a chance to work things out as well.

Recently we conducted a conflict resolution workshop with a small non-profit organization that had been arguing over a number of different plans. After almost a year of discussion they had been unable to initiate any plan of action because they had not empowered their elected leader to make executive decisions. While the leader had authority, he had no power; the group was like a football team that argued about each plan while the coach couldn't get the team on the field to start the game. Unfortunately there were too few people in this organization willing to put a plan into action and they chose to continue planning.

The increase in participation by people accelerates the "noise" level as well as the quantity of conflict. A citizen's group of Arabs and Jews in Jaffa, Israel, organize to fight for changes in the building codes for old buildings in Jaffa. Private citizens form their own navies. Greenpeace, a transnational grass roots organization, brings about changes in the policies of institutions like the International Whaling Commission. In Denver, a neighborhood of blacks and whites demonstrate before the mayor for street lights in their alleys. Power is being dispersed and rediscovered throughout all levels of social organization.

The world, as well as America, has moved beyond the image of the "melting pot." Melting into America, at first, brought about a submergence of differences and uniquenesses. Third world nations are not interested in losing their cultural identities and becoming just like the industrial nations. Many are demanding that they be considered equal partners with industrial countries in shaping their destinies.

This emergence of power in all sectors of the world family, and the willingness to use it, requires that we all reconsider traditional techniques for solving conflict as well as the responsibility that goes with power. It is important to dispel the illusion of exclusive power at the top. Misled by this illusion, and unaware of their own power, many at the grass roots level underestimate their abilities. They capitulate just at the moment they might be heard, or, like the schoolyard bully unaware of his strength, impulsively destroy the opportunity for reconciliation.

A new mandate of responsibility is emerging. Not only are leaders responsible for the use and abuse of power, but followers and dissidents as well; the relationship between them is now no longer easily distinguishable. No longer can the underdog rationalize violent and terrorist activity because he or she has less power and has been exploited. Regardless of our station in life and our level on the diagram, we all share in the responsibility and power for the welfare of the planet. There are no more scapegoats. Equal power implies equal care and responsibility.

This was illustrated on a very concrete human level when we were in Israel in March, 1984. We met one night with a young Arab political activist who had heard about our work in conflict resolution and win-win strategies. He wanted to talk to us about a conflict that had developed among the Arabs in his village which made it very difficult for them to effectively deal with the Jews. Our translator was a native born Jewish Israeli, a soldier in the army, who had fought against the Arabs in a number of Israel's wars. He was a man of utmost integrity who faithfully translated for us as we worked with this Arab to develop strategies to reconcile the differences in his village. The next morning we learned that our Jewish Israeli translator had been up most of the night struggling with himself. With tears in his eyes he confided to our group of men (Arab, Israeli, and Christian) what it was like to help an Arab come up with ways to unite his people, when he had spent most of his life as a Jewish citizen of Israel and as an Israeli soldier fighting against the Arabs. All his intellectual training told him that it was better that the Arabs remain divided, and yet here he had participated in a process of helping them become unified. In his heart he knew that it was his responsibility to help people search for a common ground.

PARTICIPATING IN CONFLICT

CHAPTER THREE

In the Wings

Every situation is unique. The best and most appropriate response in one situation at one time might be totally inappropriate in the same situation at another time. If there is any rule it might be "pay attention and be informed," knowing there is no guarantee things will work out as you hoped. We are all going to make mistakes if our primary concern is caring for ourselves and others as we participate in the search for win-win solutions.

Specific rules like "always be honest," or "never compromise," disconnect us from the immediate situation in all its complexity. This is particularly true if our rules are based on fixed beliefs and positions. For centuries people have made decisions and prescribed actions grounded on beliefs that had little correspondence to the actual situation with its many interrelationships with other situations. We can no longer afford to operate in this discrepant fashion. This places far more responsibility on us, and we need to be open to a diversity of information when making decisions.

It is necessary to stress the tentative nature of our suggestions because we have seen suggestions used at the wrong time or in the wrong place. Years ago Carl Rogers, founder of client-centered therapy, described a form of dialogue he was having with some of his clients in which he reflected back to them in a non-judgmental way what they said to him. In the context in which he worked it functioned well for him. The richness of his approach in working with his clients could hardly be subsumed under this one "technique." Yet many people imitated the "reflective response," taking it very literally and out of context. There is the story of the client who said to his therapist, "I'm going to jump out the window." The therapist reflected, "Oh, you feel like jumping out the window?" The client answered, "Yes," and jumped out the window. The therapist reflected, "Plop."

Preparation

Many people operate with the idea that there is something magical about meetings, and that if you gather a group of people together work will get done. This idea carries over into interactions between people that are expressly designed to resolve conflict. Designing a new product for the market is often done with painstaking care, yet little thought is given to the important task of paying attention to personal human interaction. The lack of care and attention to the details of human interaction makes conflict situations appear to be very complicated and overwhelming.

We have worked with organizations and families in which meetings were called where no one had prepared an agenda for himself or anyone else. This was noticeable particularly during the sixties and seventies when the climate was one of "hanging loose" and "trusting," and the presumption was that somehow magically something would emerge. We observed college professors have one meeting after another with each other or with students and spend but five minutes or less preparing for each meeting. It was as though being structured or organized was un-American and would "interfere with creativity." Everyone acted like life was an improvisation in which we were all little Marlon Brandos stumbling out on stage and "winging it." When some poor soul asked about the purpose of the meeting or expressed some discomfort at the lack of organization, he or she was criticized for being controlling and uptight. In counseling, we find that few couples have any procedure or plan for handling conflict. Many of them have no idea how or why a fight has broken out. It is as though each party has been beamed down from the Starship Enterprise into the middle of a family dispute.

This abhorrence of planning is encouraged by our educational system, particularly in the way some teachers handle homework. They do not say to a class, "We cannot proceed until you have finished your homework." The class goes on and everyone muddles through unprepared, and the teacher pretends not to notice. One can easily come to believe that this is the way to operate. Fortunately, this attitude is mitigated by extra-curricular programs like athletics, drama, and music, where practicing and preparing is a precondition for being part of the group and what the group produces.

Lack of planning leads to "crisis management" where meetings are only called to handle momentary crises that could have been avoided. What steps do you need to take when you have become aware of an impending conflict?

Reconnaissance of Internal States

Learning that you are faced with a conflict arouses a myriad of feelings, everything from anxiety and fear to anger and hopelessness. Internal scanning can produce valuable insights that affect the way in which we handle ourselves as well as the final outcome of the conflict. Visualize your worst fear. Allow yourself the luxury of really focusing on your fearful fantasies. Pretend the worst has indeed come true and you are now out of and on the other side of the imagined catastrophe. No more cares or worries and responsibilities are plaguing you. If my worst fear is the fear of being charged with "irresponsibility" or "undesirability," I no longer have to find ways to prove I am a responsible or desirable person. A certain freedom is achieved by facing our catastrophic expectations. We release some of the excess energy that is generated when it is first learned that a conflict is coming up, and we can see more clearly how to act. This exercise is often used by actors before they go on stage and are feeling very frightened.

Anxiety can be considered a very normal charge of heightened energy without which we cannot function at optimal levels of awareness. Yet at times we have a bit more than we need; the fantasy exercise helps to reduce or redistribute the energy to more manageable levels. We are then less inclined to try, for example, to manage our fears by manipulating others into submission or by making concessions.

It is not being suggested that someone fantasize ways of acting out anger. Anger or revenge fantasies affect the body differently. They recycle and escalate in intensity, preventing one from being centered. Behind angry feelings are deeper levels of fear and pain. When people confront their fears they become centered and mobilized for constructive action. Once we have our fears and other internal states at a more manageable level we can begin to gather, clarify, and analyze as much information as we can find about the conflict situation.

Listing Intentions and Needs

Make a list of your intentions: what you wish to achieve in the approaching conflict situation. Make the list as comprehensive as possible. Don't worry if at this point some of the intentions appear to conflict with each other. The following example list indicates apparently inconsistent intentions.

SOME INTENTIONS

"to prove I'm right"

"to get an education"

"to discredit someone"

"to protect my family"

"to impress people"

After you have made your list of intentions go on to make a second list of as many of your needs as possible. List those you wish to get met as well as those that may be affected positively or negatively by the conflict.

SOME NEEDS

"to feel better"

"to feel safe"

"to feel respected or understood"

"to have privacy"

"to have more friends"

Now that you have both lists go back and look to see if your needs and intentions complement each other or interfere with each other. For instance, the intention "to prove we are right" may interfere with the need "to have a safe place to live" which would require cooperative behavior with someone you are in conflict with. Imagine entering a dispute with a landlord. The need for shelter is currently being met and a conflict with the landlord could either increase your sense of security about a need for shelter or decrease it.

Three important reasons for going through this tedious task of list making are that (1) it gives us an opportunity to clarify to ourselves our needs and intentions, (2) we have a chance to look for both correspondence and contradictions that may exist, and (3) we may discover intentions and needs that really do not belong to the specific conflict situation we are entering. In our consulting work with organizations, for example, we have found that some people try to meet very personal needs that may not fit a given setting. Once we were mediating a conflict situation between nurses, social workers, and doctors in a mental health clinic. One of the social workers became aware that he had wanted a close personal relationship with the director. He had been angry and disappointed that the director, an older man, was not available for that kind of relationship. Once this became clear he and the director, both dedicated professionals, were able to focus more clearly on some ways to improve their organization.

Hidden Agendas

During the first two weeks of a Human Communication class, the instructor, one of the authors, noticed a student sitting in the back of the room with a cynical and dissatisfied expression on his face. The instructor thought the student's mood would pass as he accommodated his own expectations with those designed into the class. But instead he managed through verbal and non-verbal behavior, by not participating and by disrupting the class, to invite other students to collaborate with him and thus form a sort of underground of support. Drawing others in, he was creating a war between the class and the instructor. One day the instructor spoke with the student after class. They both acknowledged that this situation would not disappear by itself. The instructor said that he had observed the student's dissatisfaction and asked him about his intentions, goals, and expectations for the class. The instructor also described his own agenda. The cynical, disappointed look faded from the student's face once the invitation to share expectations was offered non-judgmentally. After this encounter he began to cooperate. What he needed was recognition of his own personal agenda for the class and a firm personal challenge. He received both. Before the discussion the student had said he was only in the class to get the credit and fulfill some requirements, but afterwards he professed thanks to the instructor for not criticizing those original reasons. The student then became one of the class's most productive members, and his previously haphazardly done assignments were transformed into beautiful pieces.

An agenda need not remain hidden if one is aware of what is going on beneath the superficial levels of form and notices the process. Over ninety percent of what is being communicated in any transaction is at a non-verbal level.

Invitations to Conflict

We all receive many invitations to participate in conflict situations. In ongoing conflicts a good deal is already happening that we know nothing about. When we enter we are invited sooner or later to play various roles which are seldom helpful in resolving conflict within a win-win framework. These invitations are rarely overtly stated, and if we are not careful we can find ourselves "in the soup," swimming for the side of the bowl and wondering, "How did I get here?"

For example, you are having dinner with friends—one turns to you and "innocently" asks, "Don't you think women's lib has gone too far?" Here's an invitation, but to what? A simple opportunity to share opinions? Or maybe an invitation to have you side with one of your friends against another in some ongoing dispute they have not resolved? You may have been invited to join a private dispute where two of you will gang up on a third.

Often the authors are invited to speak or consult with organizations about particular topics. The invitation is usually offered by someone within the organization who has some vague idea of our opinions. Before we arrive we are often told something like, "The staff here is really interested in learning about communication," or about "how to work with difficult families," or some other topic about which the inviter thinks we know something. On the surface this seems like a simple situation where we are going to give information to willing listeners who wish to learn more. Seldom is this the case. Invariably there is the hope on someone's part that we, because we are "expert consultants," will help one group convince another group to change or give up their position. If we were to take sides in this covert dispute we would polarize the groups, increasing the level of conflict, and prevent them from reaching some form of resolution.

A number of years ago we were invited to Israel to conduct a training workshop on Gestalt psychology and family therapy. This group united and attacked us by not participating or continually interrupting in order to cover up their internal conflicts. Fortunately, for us as well as them, we declined to enter an adversarial relationship with them. All of us were then able to address some of the underlying issues, the most important of which was the group's fear that their leader, an old man in ill health, was rapidly approaching his death, and the group was unsure about how they would be able to get on without him.

We need to let go of assumptions that what we are being invited to is simple and clear, and try to find out why we are being invited. This is not to suggest the inviters are dishonest or devious, which is rarely the case. Many times they have simply not clarified for themselves why they have invited us. Once we have clarified for ourselves the nature of the invitation we can choose whether or not we wish to accept it. Here are some examples of common invitational language and some ways it can be briefly clarified.

"Would you do me a favor?" *Clarification:* "I don't know. It depends on the favor you are asking."

"Do you want to . . . ?" This may be an innocent question or a hidden invitation to "Would you . . . ?" *Clarification:* "Would you accept a no?"

"The weather is nice, isn't it?" This sounds like an invitation to agree. *Clarification:* "Are you wondering if I am enjoying it?"

"Do you always wear your hair like that?" Is this a setup for a criticism or an observation? *Clarification:* "Do you really want to know and how come?"

"What is your opinion?" or "What do you think about that?" At this point we do not know what this person really wants to know. Does he or she want to know in order to find an opportunity to gain agreement, or is the plan to assert an opinion by attacking ours. *Clarification:* "In what way could my opinion be useful to you?" or "I'm willing to share my opinion but first I would like to hear what your opinion is."

Invitations do not have to be accepted. Years ago we were running a play therapy group with boys aged eight to eleven. There was a great deal of pushing and shoving and a number of fights. We found ourselves spending a lot of time setting limits and basically playing policemen. One day we decided to drop out of this rather unpleasant role and we informed the group that we would no longer rescue them or referee their fights. We would be there to administer first aid or listen to how they felt about what was going on. At first they did not believe us and had to test us out. When they discovered we were serious they quit fighting and sat down among themselves to make their own rules for fighting. The rules were very appropriate, and once we let go of our responsibility for making rules they were able to take responsibility for themselves. Everyone benefited from the new arrangement. We dropped out of the conflict and refused to reenter it. In fact, refusing to participate can sometimes be helpful in either bringing about a quick resolution or totally defusing the conflict.

Any plan, whether it be to decline or to enter a conflict that does not respect the need for everyone involved to maintain a sense of mutual dignity and self-respect, will lead to more struggle and to win-lose or lose-lose outcomes. To avoid rushing into a situation impulsively and unprepared, it is valuable to be in a balanced and grounded state in one's body and mind, with a minimal need to impress others with how effective you are as a resolver. Sometimes the most effective resolvers, those who can establish the greatest harmony among others, do not go around doing it as a profession or as an avocation; it comes, after much training, naturally to them.

Our aikido instructor was once with a group of friends walking in the streets of Detroit. His friends went into a store and he saw a group of youths watching and then approaching him. He tried to avoid them but couldn't since the traffic kept him from crossing the street. They came closer and asked him for ninety cents. "Ninety cents!" he said, musing on inflation and remembering a time he was asked for a quarter. Feeling quite comfortable with the group he hesitated for a moment, fumbled in his pocket and found a piece of candy. Facing the group leader he placed it in his hand and said, "Stay sweet, Baby." They walked on laughing, entertained by the response. They had accepted the remark as a confident and clever gesture from an equal.

Practicing the Art of Listening

Learning to listen well requires not only practice but some guidelines on *what* to listen for. Most of the time when someone is talking the listener is only partially listening. This means paying just enough attention so that you know when it is your turn to talk, or selecting some word, phrase, or theme out of the stream of sound coming at you so you can rehearse your response silently in your head until the sounds stop and it's your turn. When conversations occur at this level they are minimally effective. At best, the person who speaks next is talking about something that is in the general "ball park" of what the last person was talking about. Yet it is a far cry from active listening where all your attention is very focused on what is coming through from the other person, as well as what you yourself are saying.

The process of listening, though, does not flow in a uniform pattern; it is a complex transaction. When we are listening to someone else intently, thoughts and feelings are triggered in us.

We are always listening to at least two people, the other person and ourself; and it is for this reason that we need to consider internal interruptions.

They cannot be avoided or eliminated by making rules that no one will interrupt. The issue becomes "when is it all right to let your partner know that you need a break?" When internal interruptions are interfering with your listening and you cannot receive someone's feelings or point of view, you may need to tell the other person to slow down or stop before they have completely finished so you can notice the thoughts and feelings that are arising in you. This is a different kind of interruption than abruptly jumping into a conversation and sharing your thoughts and feelings. When we do that we are demanding that the other person shift from talking to listening almost instantaneously. Most of us cannot shift gears that fast, although there are times when we think we can. The rapid-fire exchange that sometimes occurs at parties where people are exchanging jokes and small talk is fun and highly stimulating, and like a good card game, sufficient unto itself. But that form of communication is not appropriate when people are trying to accomplish something.

While we can take responsibility for letting the speaker know whether or not we are listening, the speaker can also take responsibility to find out if he is being heard.

In the case of a couple, both often feel that the other is never listening, yet one will communicate important information when the other is not listening. For instance, the wife may be in the kitchen cooking and feeding a child when the husband comes home and tells her about some need of his. She says, "Uh huh," and goes on cooking. She wasn't listening. She repeats the pattern when she asks him for something while he is engrossed in some project such as balancing the checkbook, and isn't listening. They both feel that the other is not listening, and they are both right. They chose to speak when they did not yet have the other's attention.

Selective Listening

When someone has our attention this does not guarantee that we will listen to them in the way they would like. We all have our favorite ways of listening. Some people listen more carefully for feelings and intentions, others for interpretations or actions. Each of us is inclined to listen more attentively to certain kinds of information. When we do, however, we eliminate important information that might be useful in dealing with conflict. If we listen, for example, to reinforce someone's intention to be judgmental or appeasing we may be colluding in the support of a point of view or an interpretation that is not at all helpful in resolving a difficulty. Imagine listening in this way when someone says, "I really told George off for challenging me . . . don't you think I was right in doing so?" A typical response might be, "You were certainly right to do that, no one should have to take such an insult." A listener who focuses on feelings alone might respond in another way: "I can see you were really sore with him for doing that, yet you seem unsure whether you wanted to tell him off." If we listen for one kind of information alone — say, feelings — we can easily miss other equally important kinds of information.

When we sense another listening to us selectively, something useful can be done to get back in harmony with them. If someone says, "I'm really having a terrible time," we do not have to feel impelled to offer an interpretation or advise a plan of action unless that is what it is best to offer. We might start by asking, "Why is this person telling us this story?" Do they want our advice and help, our judgment and interpretation? Then we need to decide if we want to give it. Will it lead to a destructive collusion or will it bring about a positive outcome for both parties? There are many situations where it is appropriate to tell someone what to do, to judge and interpret. Any of these modes has its proper place. They often need to be made explicit so an appropriately responsible choice to be congruent or incongruent can be made by the speaker and the listener.

Here is an example of a speaker's intentions clashing with those of the listener.

Speaker: "I felt really bad about myself when I did that." The intention is to have the listener understand how the speaker felt.

Listener: "You don't have to feel that way." The intention is to rescue the speaker from his unpleasant feeling.

Here is an example of when the speaker's intentions were congruent with those of the listener. The speaker's intent is to communicate feelings and the listener is listening for feelings and responding to that component of the speaker's communication.

Speaker: "I felt really bad about myself when I did that."

Listener: "I can see why. I would also feel that way had I compromised my integrity."

There is no single correct way to listen effectively. There are many ways to listen and we need to choose that which is most appropriate in a given situation and not just go on listening in our favorite mode and be stuck there, like the psychiatrists in the elevator where one says, "It's a nice day," and the other says, when the first has gotten off, "I wonder what he meant by that."

On the next page is a short test you can give yourself to help discover your favorite mode of listening in order to increase your listening options.

LISTENING OPTIONS

NEVER SELDOM OFTEN ALWAYS

1. I ___ ___ ___ ___ give advice.

2. I ___ ___ ___ ___ give interpretations.

3. I ___ ___ ___ ___ point out details.

4. I ___ ___ ___ ___ listen for intentions.

5. I ___ ___ ___ ___ listen for a way to help or rescue.

6. I ___ ___ ___ ___ listen for feelings.

7. I ___ ___ ___ ___ listen for hidden meanings or intentions.

8. I ___ ___ ___ ___ listen for what I like or don't like.

9. I ___ ___ ___ ___ judge things good or bad.

10. I ___ ___ ___ ___ Listen for complexity or simplicity.

11. I ___ ___ ___ ___ listen for agreement or disagreement.

12. I ___ ___ ___ ___ listen for connections, patterns, or themes.

Listening for Feelings

Without words to label feelings we can miss very important information. Asking people to listen for feelings does not help much
if they have no words to describe feeling states. We have heard
therapists ask clients what they were feeling and the client respond
with either "I don't know," or express an opinion, like "I feel my
wife should clean the house." These clients were not necessarily
out of touch with their feelings or ignoring the question. Most
of us are trained in our culture to focus on learning about objects,
interpreting events, and expressing opinions. We are exceedingly
good at these tasks. Many people are embarrassed if they do not
have an opinion about something. In fact, the question "How
do you feel about so and so?" usually elicits an opinion. It is a
rare person who, when asked by a reporter, "How did you feel
about so and so being elected mayor?" responds simply with "I
was scared," "disgusted," "happy," or "sick." Without vocabulary
for feelings it is hard to explore and understand the needs of
others. In conflict resolution this is a very real barrier. The following is a list of some words that describe internal feeling states.

FEELING STATES

angry	daring	hopeful
anxious	distraught	humiliated
apathetic	eager	joyful
awed	ecstatic	nervous
bored	elated	proud
calm	excited	relieved
cautious	frustrated	sad
comfortable	foolish	silly
confident	glad	uneasy
confused	greedy	uncomfortable
contented	grieved	weary
	hesitant	

Feelings are often confused with opinions, judgments, and ideas. Describing a genuine feeling state will bring one closer to expressing one's actual needs in a conflict situation and arriving at solutions that match. When a company "feels its customers should be handled more promptly" that is only what the company *thinks*. "The administration *feels* that the faculty should settle for less" is an opinion. There is a difference between thoughts and interpretations, and emotions. It is all right to strongly emphasize something by "I feel," but what you are really saying is "I believe." One way to distinguish between thoughts and feelings is to notice whether the word "that" appears in the sentence after "I feel" — if it does, it is not an emotion that is being expressed. "I feel that you really listen to me" and "I feel that I will be able to be a good tennis player" are opinions and judgments. Appropriate feeling statements might be "I feel encouraged about my tennis playing" or "I feel comfortable when you listen to me."

In this chapter we have discussed ways to prepare ourselves to enter a conflict, and have described some skills like listening that are necessary in making this possible. Frequently we find ourselves swept into conflict so quickly that we are unable to step outside to look around, and are ill-prepared for what confronts us. Until we regain our balance we can't even begin to focus on the issues that need to be addressed. In the next chapter we will focus more directly on ways of coping with conflict once we are actually involved.

CHAPTER FOUR

Interacting in the Process

The focus in this chapter will be on what occurs when people are in an interaction process in a conflict situation. It is helpful to think of "process" as something going on in a system. On the simplest level a social system is made up of a minimum of two people who are in some sort of relationship over time in a given setting, like a man and woman living in a cabin in the mountains for five years. Let's suppose, for a minute, that this particular system is relatively stable over time and that what happens on a day-to-day basis (the process) is fairly predictable. A new person enters this system and we have a new system with a new climate and a new process. The old system has not changed. It no longer exists.

Process is a sequence of events that leads to a predictable outcome. We intuitively understand it, we infer it, participate in it, and often create it. Processes which most of us are familiar with include the disease process and the growth process. In the disease process certain symptoms take on an increasingly obvious pattern leading to a gradual deterioration of the body. In the growth process, from childhood to adulthood, there are predictable events that occur at certain times in life such as the change of voice when a male child enters adolescence. It is through the appearance of the order of certain events over time that we become aware that a process is taking place. We also know that by various interventions we can affect the direction of these processes. Many medical procedures change the course of the disease process and can reverse its direction. We can also affect the course of the growth process by adding or subtracting certain nutrients.

What is important in focusing on the process level when viewing conflict situations is that the emphasis is shifted from trying to change or alter the basic character of people to offering alternative ways people can participate in conflict. This opens up the opportunity for resolutions that avoid excess destructiveness and waste. Once we acknowledge the existence of social systems and our roles in them, changing our way of participating in a system is far easier. What follows are suggestions of ways to acknowledge and alter our participation in the conflict situation.

Trust and the Climate of Safety

In any conflict situation our first concern is how safe we are. What is this place like? Can we count on anyone for help in meeting our needs? Our early experiences tell us how safe we may feel. However unsafe we have felt in the past, trust, the ground of safety, can be rebuilt. We can let people know, for example, where we are going and when we will return, what our agendas are for them, and what we expect of them. This will tend to avoid sudden unpleasant surprises, and will create a climate of safety.

Another way to build trust is to prevent the confusion that comes from mixed messages. A mixed message is often a disparity between words and actions. We count on the consistency, for example, between verbal and non-verbal messages. We have done so since childhood. We sensed that something was wrong when we saw our mother clenching her jaw and mopping the kitchen floor furiously. However, when Mom or Dad tersely said, "Nothing," when we asked, "What is the trouble?" we felt the inconsistency, became mistrustful, felt unsafe, and went away wondering if we had done something wrong. Mixed messages, like disingenuous encounters, create a climate of distrust. The essence of what is going on is being masked. We know this from our adult experience when someone feigns patience, concern, or cooperation. Mixed messages eradicate safety and love. Therefore, being honest is a vital ingredient in a relationship that is non-conflictive. That is not to say that honesty implies total openness and that without it trust cannot be built. What is essential is that we be open about our reservations. In the above example, to say that "nothing is the matter" when something is bothering us takes away the confidence another can have in us. As a general rule we have to decide when it is appropriate to open our inner world to another, but dishonesty about our doubts and misgivings, as well as our appreciation and thankfulness, is going to lead to a closed and insecure climate. Resolutions that take place in this climate are watered down and end in compromise and stalemate. Moreover, in a closed and non-trusting climate we become distant from one another and cannot learn about each other's needs.

Vulnerability, Security Operations, and Self-Esteem

When we are in a conflict situation our self-esteem is on the line, and we come to see how weak or strong it is. In a conflict we are vulnerable and can exploit or be exploited more easily. Our weak points or vulnerabilities usually stem from the suffering brought about by earlier injury. We often cover up those injuries with "security operations," which, if not attended to, interrupt the flow of human communication. A security operation is a mobilization of defensive behavior to reestablish self-esteem when a weak spot has been touched. It is similar to what Harry Stack Sullivan described as a behavior we engage in automatically to cover up our vulnerability, such as boasting, bragging, threatening, daydreaming, or forgetting. When we or someone else shifts into a security operation it is unproductive to try to continue with what was going on before. A security operation is a public emergency and we need to attend to it by:

A. Adjusting our behavior by

    1. stopping what we are doing

    2. backing off

    3. attending to what has been triggered within us

B. Acknowledging

    1. our own security operations

    2. security operations of others

    3. taking responsibility for our own behavior

    4. apologizing

It is not an admission of guilt if we have unwittingly or wittingly hit someone's vulnerability; it is a recognition of one's power to be insensitive to the well-being of others and to injure them. If we injure someone else consciously, we are engaged in our own security operation and need to step back to look at the state of our own self-esteem. *Our most valuable and fundamental tool for conflict resolution is ourself.* While we may not be responsible for the "cause" of our weaknesses and old wounds, we cannot begin to heal them if we do not claim them and take responsibility for healing them. In the arena of world affairs this has important implications. In the Middle East, for example, anyone who demands compensation and retribution is in effect insisting on historical justification in order to not take responsibility for what they can and must do—heal themselves. That is not to discount the relevance of desires for compensation and retribution as well as the help others can give by participating in the healing process.

The importance on the international scene of adjusting our behavior and acknowledging security operations can be understood in the following example. In the spring of 1984 a group of American and Latin American scholars were writing an important foreign policy report on American involvement in Latin American conflicts. One of the authors was acting as a facilitator to this meeting, which had on its agenda the issue of non-violent conflict resolution. Early in the afternoon one member became very angry and pessimistic. The rest of the group expressed frustration at his "uncooperative behavior." The topic of violent conflict had triggered some unacknowledged feelings of pain and grief not only in the man who became angry and pessimistic but in the entire group. This quickly led to angry attacks, criticism, and a questioning of the value of what they were trying to do. All of these behaviors were significant security operations mobilized to protect the self-esteem of the group. Useful dialogue began to break down and the agreed upon task was in danger of not being completed. The author asked them if there were some old grievances or wounds that had not been addressed. It became evident that everyone in the room had recently suffered a loss. They had all lost either a colleague or friend who had been killed or who had disappeared in recent fighting. Once this pain and sorrow was acknowledged they were all able to return to writing the report.

Constructive Approaches to Criticism and Attacks

Criticism and attacks are security operations that arise in conflict situations when people begin to argue with one another over positions and beliefs. We have suggested the necessity of adjusting our behavior and acknowledging security operations. There are other approaches that do not involve looking at the state of our own self-esteem, but which depend upon a high level of self-esteem. Don't attack back or defend yourself or your character. The attacker is not an enemy. He is a vulnerable person who is attacking because of a perceived misunderstanding or threat. More often than not, counterattacks lead to an escalation of animosity and aggressive behavior and lower self-esteem.

Take the time to determine if the attack really bothers you. Some attacks on your character really don't affect you or have to affect you very much. Moreover, consider that an attack is a reflection of the feelings and attitudes the other person is struggling with. Or ignore it, thank the speaker for his opinion or perception, and get back to the subject. For example, a car is blocking another car in a parking lot. The person needing to get out asks the other to move his car. The other driver responds: "Why are *you* parked in the wrong place?" (the tone is critical and sarcastic). The first driver replies: "I'm sorry, would you please move your car."

Sometimes the attack is valid and what the attacker may not realize is that the comment about you is one you are comfortable with. So you might agree and say, "Yes, I am sometimes like that." For instance, someone might attack by saying, "You are really a silly person." A valid response can be, "Yes, I can certainly be that way."

If the attack is valid and is causing conflict in your relations with others, know that at any time, whenever it is needed, you can defend yourself in a firm way without attacking back. If what you are doing and being attacked for turns out all right, swearing on a stack of Bibles to prove you are right is a wasteful use of time.

The Value of Interpretations

If you want to waste a lot of time and escalate a conflict, tell the people you are struggling with that you know why they are doing something you don't like, i.e., "You are not listening to me *because* you only care about yourself." Even if you are right and that is the person's attitude he is not likely to take kindly to your analysis and is unlikely to acknowledge you as an expert on his intrapsychic processes. If we have learned anything from our clients it is that they are the main experts on themselves and we are the students.

This widespread habit of jumping in to interpret and theorize has roots in our early experiences in school. Many adults as children are treated as dumb and begin to believe they are. When they are asked a question and respond with "I don't know" the adult who asked the question often jumps in to provide the answer, implying that the child is unable to think about the question or explore and experiment to find the answer. Even more destructive are interruptive responses that tell the child they should have known the answer without having had to learn it. Teacher: "You don't know that yet? You should know that." This may be followed by an upraised eyebrow which encourages laughter from the other children. This, of course, can make asking questions a dangerous threat to one's self-esteem. It is a rare person who has gone through school and not indirectly learned or come to firmly believe that there is such a thing as a dumb question.

We recently came across some State Department internal communications about a meeting between some Russian and American officials that was full of amateur psychologizing about why the Russians had acted in a particular way. Our speculation is that none of the Americans asked the Russians why they were acting that way, and even if they had lied the Americans would have gained more information. It is important to keep theories private and overcome inhibitions about asking questions. Give the people you are in conflict with an opportunity to teach you about themselves.

With the increase in contacts between people from different cultures worldwide, leaving our pet theories and interpretations behind is very important. In our own work in Israel and Egypt the main thing we found helpful was an open mind and a willingness to listen and be educated. Most of the advice and interpretations we received from supposed experts we found useless. Before going to Egypt we were warned about how hard it was to get anything done because the Egyptians were lazy or had some mysterious concept about Middle Eastern time. These biases were offered to us by people in the American foreign service. It was hard to arrange meetings in Cairo, not because of differences in the "psychology of Egyptians," but because of environmental factors such as a deteriorating phone system and a transportation system that barely functioned. Everyone was affected, Egyptians and foreigners alike. Many of the Egyptian business and government people we met worked twelve to sixteen hours a day and were daily overcoming obstacles that few Americans or Europeans ever have to contend with.

Among the Arab population of Israel we failed to discover the "Arab mind." Each person was a unique human being like ourselves. We met with Moslems who had less in common with other Moslems than they did with some of their Jewish neighbors. There are as many "kinds" of Jews and Moslems as there are Christians in any American city. And we have yet to discover the "Russian soul" in the Russians we have met. Russian engineers seem to approach problems in ways similar to American, French, and German engineers.

Nixon liked the Chinese leader Zhou Enlai because he acted in ways Nixon admired, which was fortunate for both the Chinese and American citizens who benefited from the closer ties between the two countries. Nixon thought of Zhou Enlai as "possessing mature self-confidence." Nixon contrasted this with his opinion of the Russians who he felt were always trying "to prove their manhood before his aides." Russians and Chinese obviously express themselves somewhat differently, yet to conclude that one form of expression is mature and the other is immature can certainly muddy the waters in conflict resolution work.

We are not suggesting that one form of expression is better than another. On the contrary. One of the authors comes from an Irish background and the other from a European Jewish background. We each have our own peculiar form of expression, but the underlying concerns and needs are the same. Many people in conflict get distracted by the way in which someone presents himself and find it difficult to move beyond this to deeper levels of our common humanity.

A few years ago we visited a Bedouin encampment in the Negev desert at night. We needed a letter from the tribal chief whom we had not met before. Now this particular man's style was to tell stories and allegories to make his point. Our European guide's style was to "get down to business and not waste time." Every time the guide tried to force the issue the Bedouin changed the subject and told another story. We intervened and also began to tell stories and soon we all were swapping stories. This went on for hours and the women continued to bring out more food. We never discussed the letter directly but later the Bedouin leader had it ready for us.

Fear—A Process Leading to Violence

Some of our most hostile and aggressive acts, including threats and bribes, are born of fear. Fear is an obstacle to freedom and it is also our teacher and ally. Choosing to learn from fear can move us to a new balance point, a place beyond our internal struggle with choice.

In Israel, the Arabs of Nazareth were reacting to recent provocations by radical Jews who were trying to prevent them from moving into upper Nazareth. The long-range plan of these Jews was to evacuate all of the Arabs from Nazareth and, beyond that, from Israel. They had a specific fear that was driving them to terrorize lower Nazareth. The fear was that if the Arabs over-populated lower Nazareth they would eventually want to take over upper Nazareth, which is mostly Jewish. Whenever a group wants something as badly as did Prevent, the anti-Arab organization of Nazareth, the group will feel threatened and worry that they may not attain their objectives. Fear is bound up with want and desire. To know and experience one is to know and experience the other.

The Arabs also were afraid. They had a fear of being unable to counteract the forces of Prevent because of the dogmatic and persuasive power of its leadership. They were scheduled to be in a debate with the group but were afraid they would not be heard or understood by the TV audience. This desire so immobilized them that they could not enter the debate.

We spent hours working with the Arab leadership to enable them to deal with their perceived helplessness. We role played with them and came up with alternative ways of handling Prevent. All to no avail. The Arab group rejected our suggestions and gave wonderful reasons why each alternative would fail. They were afraid of doing nothing and of doing anything, and they were in conflict about what choices they had. We stopped suggesting alternatives and asked them to come up with one suggestion of a way to handle Prevent. And they did.

They decided to hold up a sign and flash it up on the screen each time the camera turned on them when it was their turn. The sign read, "Who can talk to a man like this?" The way in which we allowed them to become more fully aware of their fear was to stop suggesting alternatives and say to them that this state of confusion and helplessness they were in was perhaps more hopeless and immobilizing than any one of them even realized. By finally offering not to rescue them and argue them down, they became stimulated to create a way of handling their fear.

We must face our fear in order to see how it removes us from thinking and acting freely, from seeing more possibilities, from doing the best, least volatile thing in a situation. Only in this way can all the needs of people be met and harmony established without sacrifice or compromise.

Watching our fear from moment to moment, if we are not in immediate danger that calls for action, is a luxury we can afford. We can learn how fear controls us in a conflict situation as we become intimately aware of our inner sensations, our words, our tone, and how we organize our thoughts and actions in response to someone we are in conflict with. Seeing fear move within us produces a change. The awareness itself releases tension and frees us to act. By living with the fear from moment to moment we see how it comes up and how it intricately affects our relationships with others, and this produces change.

Being in the Middle

Sometimes an individual or a nation is in the middle between two parties who are in conflict. While this middle position allows one to see both sides of a conflict with some appreciation of what each side wants, it is not a neutral position. How the conflict gets resolved is going to affect the middle man's vested interests. In typical win-lose scenarios the third party (Dad, Mom, a lawyer, a diplomat), the one in the middle, tries to pressure one or both sides into making concessions through threats or bribes; or, as so often happens, the person in the middle joins one side against the other. This is risky for the person in the middle. Both sides could also compete for the support and protection of the third party, or in the end turn against him. The third party might also be tempted to turn against either side or give up on them. These scenarios perpetuate conflict rather than end it.

Peacemakers sometimes choose the middle position. The stance of neutrality is not one of strength and engenders justified suspicion in other people, particularly when in a life and death conflict. When the third party makes explicit its own interests, however, a conflict between two parties is more honestly seen for what it is, a three-way conflict in which all stand to gain or lose. Once this is acknowledged the doors are open for seeking options that are win-win-win. A pretense of neutrality or altruism is seldom believed for long and perpetuates a continued state of distrust. Steering a middle path has its value for information gathering and for reaching a resolution if win-win rules are followed; but it in no way releases us from honestly facing our own vested interests and the risks in holding them.

SOME SUGGESTIONS

**Observe and notice the differences between the sides.
Find out what your own interests are.
Assess the risk-loss factors.**

Mind Reading

Mind reading, like an attack, also presents important choices. Mind reading sounds like this: "I know what you are thinking, you can't fool me . . . I can read you like a book." "You are not serious . . . you are stalling." "What you need is. . . . "

Don't argue or defend yourself by denying what the person has said. This provokes resistance and leads nowhere. *Do* ask yourself if there is any truth to what the mind reader said. If there is you can admit that you may have entertained such thoughts at one time or another. Or again, you may ignore the remark. If the hard-playing mind reader is insistent, you can ask if there is much point in continuing to communicate. If the mind reader does not feel he or she needs you to communicate because of his or her ability to read minds, you might say, "I am willing to get out of the way so you can do this and I invite you to carry on by yourself." If it is in a group situation you may want to invite the mind reader to conduct the meeting by himself without the participation of the group.

If the mind reader persists you can just sit silently and watch. During this silence you can use the time productively to think of ways that will facilitate what you have set out to do by being at the meeting. It is your responsibility to stay on track even if everyone else has momentarily fallen off.

The mind reader is demonstrating that he or she does not trust you. The process of communicating has broken down and he or she is raising the issue of trust. No amount of argumentation will regain lost trust. The appropriate question for you to ask is, "What action would be necessary for you to regain trust?" And this can be negotiated.

PART THREE

A CONFLICT RESOLUTION WORKSHOP

CHAPTER FIVE

Thinking on the Run

**When you are in the field of action you
have to do your thinking on the run.**

Saul Alinsky

Our workshop model contains some unique features that contribute to developing an understanding of conflict. The model provides a context for learning on an intimate group level, and increases the amount that can be learned in a short period of time. While the specific contents are extremely important, the sequence in which they are experienced is crucial in establishing a foundation at every stage so that what is learned at the next stage has firm support. This then enables the participants to have a solid understanding of the win-win approach by the end of the workshop.

Central to the workshop model is the daily practice of the martial art aikido by all the workshop participants. Aikido is used because it is an opportunity for groups that are in conflict to work together each day at a task that is demanding, non-competitive, and involves physical contact.

Aikido is a defensive martial art where there is no room for competition involving strength vs. weakness, winners vs. losers, and right vs. wrong. With practice, its techniques increase our awareness of ourselves, our partners, and our surroundings for the purpose of becoming more resourceful and alert in everyday life, particularly in situations of stress and conflict. In its highest application it is a way of life designed to train mind and body to live a peaceful and happy life by blending with opposition and crisis.

Trust and Honesty

We do not fight one another in aikido. Instead we learn trust and harmonious movement. What initially appears combative, and could become so if one had a fighting mind, is transformed into a graceful and unified dance. The movements in aikido require that we not use force or strength if they are to be effective. And this demands that we trust in our ability to use power in a coordinated and honest fashion, e.g., bending the wrist the way it wants to go, not in the opposite direction. When delivering or receiving a strike, if we mistrust ourselves or the other, hold back or try to overpower the striker, the movement fails to work and leads nowhere. However, if we blend with the attack and without strength deflect its force or aggression, we have made harmony and defused a potentially dangerous situation.

Power and Force

There is a clear distinction between power and force in aikido. Power comes from being in a calm, alert, and grounded state; force does not. A grounded state in aikido is achieved when you stand low, concentrate on a point beneath the navel, and relax to keep balance. Power with harmonious intention, the intention to reconcile in a loving way, is different from power that is combative or forceful. Practicing together over and over again, delivering techniques and receiving them, we gain more confidence as leaders and followers and begin to experience trust and power without giving or receiving injury or winning and losing.

In aikido, there are some basic attitudes which when practiced make harmonious living an everyday reality.

Non-resistance. Every day we practice resistance. We enter into contests and arguments where we force, fight, and oppose one another. What we find is that someone will always be stronger. One of the points of learning non-resistance is that you use another's strength to produce effective movement and action rather than counter it. We use it by seeing where it came from and where it wants to go naturally. The other person moves us, leads us into what to do next. Aikido provides ways to not fight back through maintaining a low center of gravity, blending, and good timing. These methods will also help us cope if we are attacked physically or emotionally.

Leading and Following. Movements in aikido form a smooth and continuous exchange of giving and receiving, initiating and executing techniques. We exchange in this way to learn to be balanced on both sides of our bodies and minds and thereby learn unity and self-control. There are also specific ways to train the body to use its right and left, dominant and passive, and weak and strong side in order to achieve balance and integration of the mind and body. With practice it is hard to see where leading and following, as well as initiating and receiving, start and end; they are continuously changing.

Self-control. We learn to control our minds and bodies so we can become more calm, aware, and responsive in a crisis situation. In a crisis or conflict we must learn how to respond in a relaxed, alert, and instantaneous fashion in order to make harmony or reconcile differences with words or actions. Customarily we either try to control or are controlled by people and objects. In either case we are put off balance and then begin to compete and force our way. All aikido techniques teach us how to become one with ourselves and other persons so control is not necessary. When we are moving together and not fighting each other, smooth, fearless, and powerful movement occurs. Unified movement or action comes when we go beyond our egotistic ideals of how to move or act effectively, and instead learn how to do so naturally.

Beginner's Mind. A beginner's mind is an attitude in which junior students and senior students learn equally from one another. A junior student gives us an opportunity to find out how aggressive, egotistic, or unrefined our techniques might still be. Working with a beginner's mind is a test of humility and non-self-righteousness. It is a chance to practice care and regard for others when they are of a lower or higher rank. We are open at every moment to learn about our strengths and weaknesses, our vulnerabilities, and to trust, respect, and care for those we work with both on and off the mat (where we practice our aikido techniques).

The daily practice of aikido by all the participants is a unifying experience that continues through the entire length of the workshop. Much of the early didactic and experiential activity in the workshop is conducted in two separate homogenous groups that meet daily. This makes it possible for people to be more open and honest as they begin to explore and clarify their needs. It is difficult, as well as potentially harmful, to ask people to be vulnerable in front of those they have been in conflict with. Earlier in the history of research into group process it was thought that keeping groups in conflict together would encourage openness and toleration. It did not; it increased the possibility for injury and argumentation and participants became entrenched in their original positions. The early separation into groups avoids the opportunity for polarization and allows people to explore deeper levels of their experience. It backs the conflict away from the impasse. The impasse is that point where people in conflict argue and fight over their positions and solutions. The impasse is also that critical choice point in any conflict where the conflict can degenerate and send people off, without support, in any number of unproductive directions rather than continue in the direction of a new state of balance. The following chart illustrates some undesirable directions that can emerge from impasses during long periods of conflict.

PROCESS MODEL OF CONFLICT

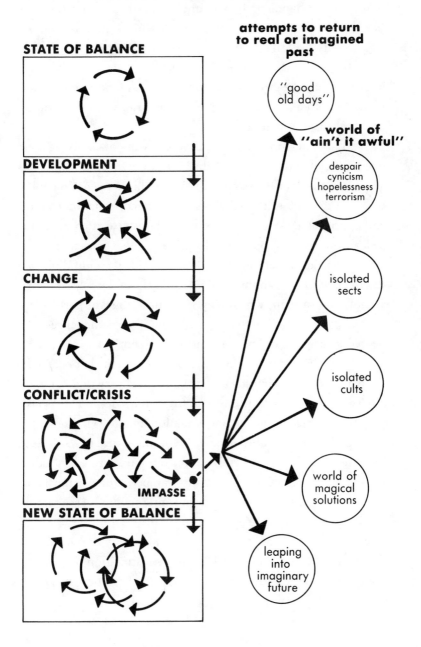

Another feature of the model is the way in which needs and solutions are handled. It is in the small groups that the participants begin to separate their needs from solutions.

Needs are analyzed according to the three need levels described in earlier chapters. The grievances are also sorted out in order to lay the groundwork for dealing with past injuries and pain. Now there is a foundation for the grief work that will be undertaken at a later stage.

Many interruptions occur as groups work at clarifying their needs. Beliefs are uncovered that interfere with our ability to accept our needs or someone else's. When this happens time must be taken to explore these beliefs. They need to be understood and appreciated. What appears to be an obstacle often turns out to lead the entire group to a deeper and more enriched level.

A particular set of beliefs that can create a lot of difficulty has to do with the symmetrical relationship of the roles of hero, victim, and dragon, which play such an important part in our personal and cultural mythology. This mythology influences how people look at needs, power, and self-esteem.

In the heroic script there are only three kinds of people in the world: heroes, victims, and dragons. It is very difficult to be a hero without a victim to rescue from some dragon. It is also possible to feel heroic in one situation in life, victimized in another, and to feel in danger of becoming a dragon. All three identities are parts of ourselves, yet the parts are often either ignored or denied. The heroic stance can perpetuate conflict and all too frequently encourage violent interactions. An example would be when national leaders speak of rescuing some group of people, the victims, from some other country that is labeled the dragon. This also interferes with consideration of win-win options or programs that are aimed at acknowledging the power people have for running their own lives.

In the extreme form of the script, heroes look for victims to rescue from dragons. Heroes believe that victims have no power or ability to take care of themselves. They need to be saved, protected, and helped.

A classic example of this is the scenario that takes place in many American hospitals every day when a woman gives birth. The woman is immobilized, her power denied and taken away, while the heroic doctors and nurses "deliver the baby" and rescue the mother from the danger of all sorts of potential pathologies, "the dragons." Fortunately, recent trends toward home births, birthing centers, and new practices and attitudes in hospitals, are providing other alternatives closer to what occurs in Holland and Sweden, where a doctor or midwife merely assists a woman to carry out a normal function she is considered to have the power and ability to perform.

The dismal effect of the heroic script can also be seen in the failure of so many African development projects. The World Bank reported in 1983 that Western and Soviet nations pressured African governments in the 1970s to take on projects that were inappropriate in design and selection, and were too expensive and grandiose. They "contributed little to economic growth or to generating foreign exchange to service the debt." These projects are called "white elephants" by the World Bank and are part of the heroic script of donor nations. The projects are chosen for their ability to increase a nation's political prestige without regard for the needs of the indigenous population or the rate of economic return. The Russians built a cement factory with a capacity of fifty thousand tons a year and found out that the road and rail systems could not handle the output and that no markets were even located nearby. They started a meat canning plant in Somalia and did not know that Africans regard cattle as investments against future hardship, and that Somalis would rather eat fresh meat. Canadians took sixty thousand acres from the Barbaig, a pastoral people of Tanzania, and transported the tribe and its cattle into areas that are now overgrazed. The Canadians then took this land and began to develop prairie-style farms which rain storms have eroded and destroyed. Ironically, the Canadians did a similar thing in the 1930s in their own country and suffered terrible dust storm soil erosion.

It is necessary when clarifying needs to also clarify grievances. Time must be taken to explore and understand these grievances. Behind grievances are grief and pain based on losses in the present and past. The reason our workshop model creates the time and space to deal with these grievances is because there is so much potential creative energy bound up in avoiding feeling pain from losses and injuries. It is hard to accomplish much with one hand painfully tied behind your back. *Unresolved grief reduces a person's responsiveness.* Once this energy is set free people are empowered to attend to the tasks at hand.

During the first six days of the workshop the participants spend most of their time working in separate small groups. There are two important exceptions to this. The first is the daily contact during the aikido practice. The other is informal meetings in small groups consisting of four people, two from each of the larger groups. These subset groups meet every day. They have no schedule, no facilitator, and no agenda. The small mixed groups are established to form a natural bridge between the other groups. They provide an informal communication link which at a later point will be useful when both groups work together sharing and searching for new options to resolve conflict. This particular intervention, i.e., the creation of subsets, has been used successfully in a number of international conflict situations.

By the end of the sixth day, needs have been clarified and most of the grief work has been done. Before the groups can generate new options, however, one more step must be taken. This involves bringing the groups together on a symbolic level. To accomplish this a ceremonial dinner is held on the evening of the sixth day.

It is not enough to deal with loss and pain within each separate group. The pain and loss underlying the grievances of those in conflict cover a wide range — from the loss of life, land, property, job opportunities, and personal as well as nationalistic dreams. Both groups need the opportunity to find out about what the other side has experienced in relation to grievances and loss during the workshop. The way in which this is done is up to each group. There can be very creative rituals through which to share their experiences. To do this, individuals first need the privacy of their own group to deal with this pain. Then they need the distance of a gift-giving ritual in order to share with the others the meaning of injury and pain, and how it has held them back from feeling a sense of power, self-esteem, and relatedness. A ceremonial dinner reconnects people who have been separated by grief and loss. The form it takes can vary from the gift of music, poetry, dance, sculpture, drawings, songs, and improvisations of all sorts. Giving through these forms is a way to share and release the intense experiences people have undergone during the entire workshop. Art depersonalizes the emotional experience and enables the participants to gain some distance from the raw experience in order to transform it.

FICTIONALIZED DIARY OF A WORKSHOP PARTICIPANT

1st Day

I registered for the workshop this afternoon. There are twenty-four of us, twelve Arabs and twelve Jews. The facilitators are from Israel and the United States. I felt somewhat skeptical and apprehensive, not knowing what all this would come to. I saw a few people I knew. At the beginning of tonight's meeting we all got a chance to introduce ourselves. I could tell some of us felt pretty nervous during the introductions. Afterwards, though, I relaxed.

Here's our schedule and a chart about conflict that the facilitators said might help guide us through the workshop.

CONFLICT RESOLUTION WORKSHOP
DAILY SCHEDULE

1st Day **Friday:**	7–8:00 P.M.	Registration
	8:00 P.M.	General meeting (introductions by facilitators and participants)
2nd Day **Saturday:**	9:00 A.M.	General meeting (everyone will state their positions and solutions to issues they are most concerned about and the impasse will be explored)
	2:15 P.M.	Aikido (entire group)
	4:00 P.M.	Small group meetings (introduction to separation and clarification of needs)
	8:00 P.M.	General meeting (lecture demonstration of fundamentals of communication)
3rd Day **Sunday:**	9:00 A.M.	Small group meetings (continue needs clarification)
	2:15 P.M.	Aikido (entire group)
	4:00 P.M.	Small group meetings (continue needs clarification)
	8:00 P.M.	General meeting (introduction to non-verbal communication)
4th Day **Monday:**	9:00 A.M.	Small group meetings (begin work on grievances)
	2:15 P.M.	Aikido (entire group)
	4:00 P.M.	Small group meetings (continue with grievances)
	8:00 P.M.	Small groups (beginning of grief work)
5th Day **Tuesday:**	9:00 A.M.	General meeting (guest speaker—on historical background to current conflict area)
	2:15 P.M.	Aikido (entire group)
	4:00 P.M.	Small groups (continue grief work)
	8:00 P.M.	Small group meetings (continue grief work and plan how to share this with other small group)

6th Day Wednesday:	9:00 A.M.	Small group meetings (finish lists of all needs)
	2:15 P.M.	Aikido (entire group)
	4:00 P.M.	Small group meetings (groups meet alone without facilitators to plan for ceremonial evening)
	7:30 P.M.	Entire group (dinner and ceremonial evening)
7th Day Thursday:	9:00 A.M.	Aikido (entire group)
	2:30 P.M.	General meeting (time for sharing and giving feedback) No planned evening meetings
8th Day Friday:	9:00 A.M.	General meeting (lecture demonstration on organizational structures and how certain kinds facilitate generation of options and intro to networking)
	2:00 P.M.	Aikido (entire group)
	4:00 P.M.	Small group meetings (begin generation of options, brainstorming)
	8:00 P.M.	Small group meetings (continue generating options)
9th Day Saturday:	9:00 A.M.	Finish generating options and begin to get selective
	2:00 P.M.	Aikido exam (entire group and selected guests)
	4:00 P.M.	Small group meetings (select options)
	8:00 P.M.	General meeting (both groups present options)
10th Day Sunday:	9:00 A.M.	Small group meetings (consider own and other groups' options —more brainstorming)
	2:00 P.M.	General meeting (both groups present options and find specific areas they can begin to work on together, facilitators bow out)
	8:00 P.M.	Open for whatever groups want and saying goodbye

DESCRIPTIVE MODEL
FOR WIN-WIN APPROACH

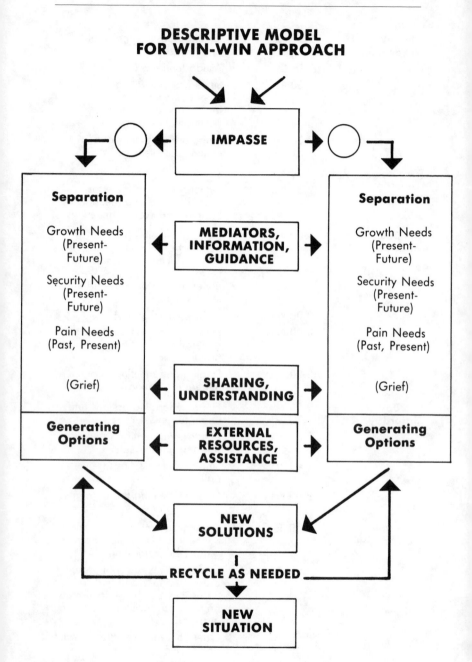

It is now later in the evening, the first meeting is over, and I am back in my room getting ready for bed. I now have a better idea with whom I am going to be spending the next ten days. When the group facilitators asked each of us to share our hopes and expectations publicly, some people hoped they would learn something but were pretty cynical. Some of the personal introductions seemed unclear. There were a few people who held opinions so different from mine that I wonder how in the world I am going to be able to communicate with them. And then there is this win-win idea. It sounds good but my past experience tells me that things in the real world just don't work out that way. Well, tomorrow morning I will have a chance to state my position and let everyone know what I think should be done. Tonight the facilitators gave each of us a wooden sword. I really wonder what that's got to do with non-violent conflict resolution.

2nd Day

This morning we met again, all together, and shared our opinions about the Arab-Jewish tensions in our respective towns. I felt relieved that this morning we didn't spend too much time rehashing and arguing. I've spent so much time in those kinds of meetings the last six months. Here are some notes I took of comments by a few of the other participants.

> **''Here we were, stating our positions, and we weren't allowed to argue with each other. I thought one person was going to jump out of her skin every time she heard something she didn't agree with.''**

> **''I felt frustrated after I stated my position. I'd stayed up half the night thinking up clever ways to defend myself, and then no one was allowed to attack me.''**

> **''I looked up at the two recording charts at the end of the morning and there was my position right there**

along with all the others. Each one was different and unique, even those from the people in my own small group.''

''If the facilitators hadn't imposed that rule about no attacking or defending we could have argued a week over many of the opinions people expressed. Half the time, the organization I belong to resembles a debating society and we never seem to get anything done.''

''I often have ideas I want to express but I never can think of how to defend them so I often just keep my mouth shut.''

''This morning's session really frustrated me. I couldn't criticize anyone, and then I began to think how little I had to say about my own position.''

''After the meeting I thought that our own small group was really going to have to get its act together if we were going to be able to take on that other group.''

''I can't remember the last time I got to say something and everyone just sat there and listened.''

''I like the excitement of a good argument. This was really boring.''

''There was one man in the other group that I was sure I wasn't going to like, but after I heard him talk he didn't seem so strange.''

We had our first aikido class. All of us lined up evenly on the edge of the mat. We were kneeling, facing our instructor. Then we bowed our heads and the instructor (or sensei) bowed back to us. I sensed a feeling of peaceful dignity in the room. In the silence I experienced a togetherness I have only felt with some of my closest friends. We bowed to the room, to the mats, to the sensei, and to each other throughout the session. The bow is to show respect and appreciation for each other. We did warm-up exercises and practiced basic movements, what the sensei called the building blocks for every technique in aikido.

The first movement we learned was a simple blending movement which is really not so simple; I may be working on it for years.

My partner, Peter, was moving toward me aggressively time and time again as I practiced the first move. Suddenly, without effort, and with considerable grace and dignity, he was beside me and we were both moving in the same direction. The direction the attack had come from was interrupted and we were unable to hurt each other. Peter, who was on the attack, was returned harmlessly to his point of origin. The attacker became my partner and followed my lead. I felt like saying to Peter, "Thank you for showing me a way that we can both move together without needing to attack."

At first this movement seemed clumsy, but after the first session I experienced greater ease and coordination in working with my partner, and without force or effort I moved more effectively and powerfully with him. The sword that I received is to be used to learn the art of self-control, timing, and dealing with our vulnerable points. Generally it is used to practice clear, unified movements of mind and body.

3rd Day

Yesterday we were divided into two small groups. All the Arabs are in one group and all the Jews in another. Our group will continue to meet throughout the ten days of the workshop. We began separating and clarifying our needs and solutions, and this continued today. The facilitators said this would help us, much later in the workshop, to explore some new options. We worked with each other to find our needs and to help each other discover ways to meet them. I noticed that again and again we demonstrated our commitment to respect each other as we struggled to discover what a need was. Even more challenging was observing how far or close our solutions were to meeting our needs. Openness, trust, and a feeling of family started to be felt among us in our small group. Our minds came back again and again to looking for simple and peaceful ways to settle things. It's a good thing we are practicing aikido each morning and learning how complexity and effort impede harmony.

4th Day

Today one participant, Noam, said he needed the government to provide more money for school books and supplies for the children of his village, especially the Arab children. We began to focus on education as a need to grow and to watch others grow and develop. Many ideas started to flow at that point — when we identified the need and changed the context from a situation that was problem-centered to that of a situation to be improved. Some of the ideas introduced were volunteer teachers, children's learning teams, book sharing, dramatizations, tutorial programs, fund raising, and a letter-writing campaign to let Americans know the facts about education for Arab children. Books were only a small part of education and the government money only one possible solution.

Another participant, Ahmed, spoke of a need for a job. The group began to list the many needs a job could meet. After he recognized that working for someone was only one option, the group helped him expand the focus beyond the job and come up with a list of multiple options for making money.

Ruth expressed the need for us all to love each other. This vague need, once clarified, was seen to refer to specific needs and actions. And then the question came up of what actions or conditions Ruth could gain control of without changing the planet first. Ruth discovered she had a lot of control over who she wanted to work with and didn't need to have everybody love her in order to get some work done.

What is the point of spending so much time clarifying needs? I learned that it was not in order to come up with a scientifically acceptable definition of needs, but to open up the possibility for new options when someone is feeling stuck. Some of the participants were focusing on very narrow solutions to meet undefined needs. Others, like Ruth, focused on very broad issues. Consequently, for some, the task became one of broadening their awareness. For others it was filling in the details in a broad landscape. Throughout the process, people were encouraged by the facilitators to respect the basic legitimacy of what they wanted regardless of how they expressed their needs.

As we were sorting out our grievances and looking at our needs and solutions, Miryom and I became very angry. She had just lost her brother in a recent terrorist attack and our family was relocated and in the process lost a lot of property. Our pain was still very fresh. Some members of the group imagined revenge for the losses we had suffered. Others, like Rena, said she wanted to just disappear into some distant past or into an imaginary future where there was no more pain. Meanwhile the present is difficult for all of us.

5th Day

This afternoon in aikido I had a major breakthrough. For days now every time I took a forward roll to the left my head would turn in the wrong direction. I felt very frustrated with myself. Today, without any effort on my part, my head just turned in the right direction. This is hard to explain. My body was doing what I wanted without my need to will it or force it. I felt absolutely exhilarated.

6th Day

Today we were not getting anywhere. A number of us felt stiff and guarded with one another and the communication seemed very formal. The facilitators decided that it was not enough to merely acknowledge the pain and loss we had experienced and they decided to lead us in a group experience. They said that there were many ways to approach the grieving process, from psychodramatic techniques to guided imagery, and that this was another approach. We were open and felt enough trust to go into this experience with them. They then led us in a grief meditation:

"Let us go together back to the source of this tension and pain, through a safe tunnel that is lit. You are guided by a protector, if you need one, until you are fully there again at the time of the loss. Can you clearly see the entire scene, everyone who was there, where they all were positioned, the sounds, the expression on their faces? Can you remember what was exchanged, what you wanted, and what you needed? What did others say and do? Can you recall feelings of helplessness and the conclusions you reached about yourself and others? Be there now for a while. Is there anything holding you back from being there as you were . . . if so, let go of it.

"Slowly begin to gain some perspective on the freedom you had and did not have, and forgive yourself for your helplessness and recognize the ways you did help, given your limits. Forgive and release others for their actions, for their fears and insecurities that were motivating them to hurt you or to remain indifferent to your needs. They were not without feeling, but those feelings may have been eclipsed by the pain and fear they were carrying around in them and acting out with you. They were immersed in their own flight-fight-fear process and exploited by their belief systems and organizations.

"You can let go of your fear, pain, and loss; let go from your heart. You will experience a cleansing action in your heart as it fills with more light, and the light may slowly push away those feelings of loss. You may come to accept those who have hurt you as misguided. The light can fill you with love and acceptance. Pure unbounded light is what surrounds us beneath these forms, beneath our personalities, our differences, the hurt, and the rage."

The grief meditation enabled me to release an incredible amount of pain and to reexperience my losses from another vantage point. The new vantage point came to me after experiencing the pain and grief behind my anger. I felt a sense of atonement, which really means at-one-ment, being at one with myself and others again. I now feel more free to pursue some new ideas and opportunities. I am denying my needs, power, and kinship with others less. It may sound hackneyed by now, but the process of forgiveness, or being at one again with those I have injured, and with those who have injured me, feels like a very important accomplishment. I never realized how feelings of grief need to be fully recognized in order to regain power and hope, and to attend to our growth and security needs.

I also realized one more thing after the grief meditation. When it comes to pain needs, to feeling helpless and vengeful, being a hero and a victim has strange advantages. When I am the hero, for instance, I can rescue others from assuming responsibility. When I do this, I disown or deny my own needs and then feel more powerless. I find myself a hero-turned-victim. Feeling helpless and vengeful is a way to manage the pain brought on by the cultural hero role I sometimes play.

In our meeting this afternoon, tears were shed as Ahmed told of a child dying in his arms. Rena stormed out and returned an hour later carrying a stray cat. She gave it to Peter, who often acts very cool and together. He held the cat and a tear rolled down his cheek. Noam gave a cup of coffee to Miryom who just sat quietly smiling. We sat there for a while in silence. Then we all slowly left the room.

In the privacy of our group we have confronted years of past pain and grievance. Now there is going to be a ceremonial dinner. All they told us was to bring some kind of gift and share with others what these past six days have been like for us. We have been working intensely, each of us, and as a group, to come up with some kind of gift we could present to describe what the workshop has meant to us so far. In addition to our individual offerings our group decided on a poetry-music presentation.

This evening we had our ceremonial dinner. The dining area gradually filled. There was laughter and some joking. People arrived with food, many different kinds. Everyone brought a gift. Ruth was sitting in a chair with a bucket of hot water at her feet and some towels in her lap. She offered to wash each person's hands. During the meal a lot of us got up and made short speeches. Joseph, who had been called "the old man," offered a large rock to the group. It was hard and heavy yet in every crevice there were tiny pieces of mica which sparkled like his eyes. Rena brought a bouquet of wild flowers she had picked and gave everyone a small handful of blossoms. When the meal was over David played his guitar and sang an old Irish ballad. Peter, who had worn his army uniform, walked out into the center of the room. He was joined by Ahmed, Noam, Ali, and Sid. At his command they began a mock battle with their wooden swords. One by one they fell to the ground. He saluted them and Miryom placed flowers in their hands. We lit a fire and everyone joined hands and danced in a circle. We all sang. As the fire died everyone wandered off into little groups. The desert air smelled clean and the stars were a little brighter.

7th Day

This morning we resumed our aikido and each person seemed lighter and more harmonious. I could see us blending more effortlessly. Opponents became partners.

In the final days of the workshop the learning seemed to proceed so rapidly I could hardly keep up with what happened in the diary entries. We have been learning very useful things about conflict resolution to take back with us to our communities. And we have been finding ways to integrate this material in terms of specific goals and commitments.

CHAPTER SIX

Generating Options

In chapter five we described the first six days of our hypothetical workshop. Our imaginary diarist ends the entries on the morning of the seventh day. From this point until the end of the workshop the groups continue to meet separately and together as they begin to concentrate on generating new options and designing procedures for implementing plans they have jointly designed. Based on our experience conducting many kinds of intensive workshops, the last two or three days are characterized by people working at very high energy levels. It is as if everyone shifts into overdrive. A four-hour session runs six hours and no one notices the passage of time. Work that under normal circumstances takes weeks happens in hours. This phenomenon of high energy performance continually renews our faith in the extraordinary potential and capacities of human beings. During this final period there are many interactions in which people can manifest and direct this tremendous influx of cooperative energy.

The early phases of the workshops lay the groundwork for this to happen if time is taken to allow for the development of trust. Trust opens the way for people to work cooperatively and become clearer in their intentions. The grief work helped to do this, and has enabled people to tap into large stores of energy. It is difficult to not feel awe and wonder at what humans are capable of when they join together working for common humanitarian goals, which is what win-win is basically all about. To grasp what we are describing, we invite the reader to recall those times when they were part of some group that made the kind of transformational shift we are alluding to. You might have been working on a stage crew in a high school play, participating as a campaign worker in the final stages of a political campaign, or as a member of a musical group in the last stages of rehearsal before opening night. What all these experiences have in common is a deadline that everyone is committed to meet, and where everyone is working together with enthusiasm to meet it. The mood is often light and humorous. Many spontaneous expressions of caring occur. People seem to lose their egos, i.e., their pride and pompousness. They laugh at themselves and with each other.

Within this overall atmosphere the participants of our imaginary workshop take on their final tasks. Here are some of the directions and structures that exist in the last stages.

Generating Options

The wellspring of our imaginations contains the deepest resources for transforming something. It contains images, metaphors, words, and plans of action. To tap into that wellspring one first has to look at the situation to be improved. It helps to call it a *situation* to be improved and not a *problem*. When we think of "problems" we at times narrow our focus and try to get rid of them. Ridding a situation of something places us in a subtractive mode of thinking. The additive process is started by reconceptualizing the problem as a possibility in which to be creative. We start to think of what to add to the situation. This is aided by brainstorming, choosing, and committing.

STEPS FOR IMPROVING A SITUATION
PROBLEM = SITUATION

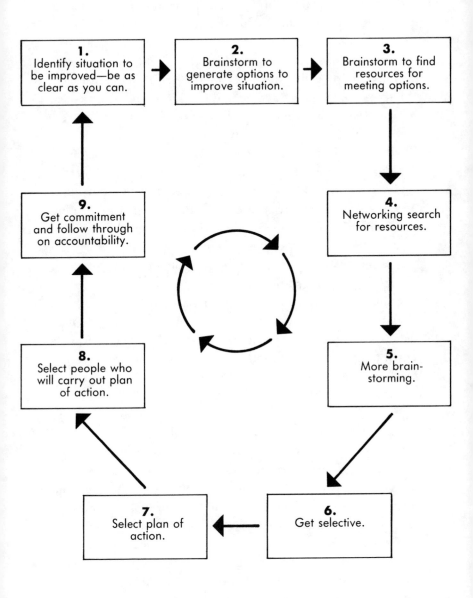

1.
Identify situation to be improved—be as clear as you can.

2.
Brainstorm to generate options to improve situation.

3.
Brainstorm to find resources for meeting options.

4.
Networking search for resources.

5.
More brain-storming.

6.
Get selective.

7.
Select plan of action.

8.
Select people who will carry out plan of action.

9.
Get commitment and follow through on accountability.

Procedures for Brainstorming

Brainstorming is a well known concept in organizations; but the specific procedures that bring it about are not, and therefore it does not become a useful tool in bringing about consensus. Brainstorming can prepare a group for consensus if participants suspend judgment so all ideas can be included. Criticizing builds distance and prevents consensus; moreover, it stifles creativity. What was said about listening and talking is true about creating and criticizing; they can rarely be done simultaneously.

The procedures for brainstorming are simple. (1) Welcome ideas, do not judge, criticize or comment on them. All ideas have their own validity. (2) Write all ideas down for everyone to see; this generates the enthusiasm and momentum necessary for the creative process. (3) Piggyback ideas, joining and combining one with another. (4) Set a specific time for breaks and resuming sessions. (5) Become selective.

One way to encourage quality as well as quantity of ideas, and to suspend judgment, is to have people enter into a meditative state of mind, a state of relaxed alertness where the focus is set beyond competition and criticism. What tends to happen then is that differences and similarities in ideas are generated for a rich harvest. The selection process is also enhanced because reaching unanimity is easier once people put aside their personalities, i.e., their favorite options and motives for those options. In the use of brainstorming and meditation for problem solving, people build off each other's ideas and a climate of respect and commitment to the legitimacy of different ideas is created.

During a one-day workshop in Israel, seventeen Jews were involved in a two-hour brainstorming session. In the afternoon the group divided in half and formed two circles, an inner and an outer circle. Each person in the inner circle had someone behind them who was to cheer whenever an idea came up. If a criticism slipped in, the outer group booed and the person who slipped was gently rapped on the shoulder. At first they were somewhat stiff and hesitant but soon the ice was broken and the ideas began to flow amid much laughter and humor. Twenty-six concrete ideas came up on how to improve Arab-Jewish relationships. The ideas included an integrated baseball league for young boys, children-swapping during summer holidays, an Arab-Jewish women's sewing group, ideas for a joint business venture, and an Arab-Jewish national holiday.

The Issue of Dissatisfaction

After a group has come up with some exciting possibilities, a point is reached when a solution is close at hand. What do you do when the group feels very happy with the work almost completed, but someone is holding out? A group can be tempted to gang up on the "holdout." If we are to keep to the spirit of win-win this is a critical point. We need to remind ourselves of a basic principle of win-win which is "all needs are to be met." If someone is still dissatisfied we have not come up with "the solution" yet; we are only part way there. The one holding out has some unmet needs that still can't be fully articulated.

All too frequently the individual is coerced into going along or living with solutions imposed by others. The reasons are many and the justifications for majority rule would fill volumes. Many popular books offer techniques to influence others to go along with us. This whole orientation closes off possibilities for finding resolutions that satisfy everyone. Those who are satisfied with the proposed solution can endanger the win-win process and the person who is dissatisfied. The dissatisfied person is hard pressed from within as well as from others to capitulate and discount his inner feelings of dissatisfaction. All kinds of self-criticism can come into play. He can believe he is unrealistic or overly critical. The person's needs for acceptance and affiliation may override his courage to ask for clarity. The members of the group must reaffirm their commitment to win-win and wait patiently for the process to complete itself.

Historically, the dissident, the eccentric, the person most sensitive to pain, has led the rest of us on to more humane levels of human interaction. We all have much to learn from the artists, the dreamers, the schizophrenics, the visionaries, and the neurotics in our midst. While it may seem inefficient to delay closure because of one "holdout," the long term benefit can be enormous. The Quaker dialogue on the issue of slavery lasted for one hundred years before it became an official position. They arrived at this position without casting any slave owner out of membership, without censoring or ostracizing anyone. One might complain that this process took too long, yet the Quakers arrived at this position one hundred years before the American Civil War and over two hundred years before the Freedom Riders of the 1960s. We are not just suggesting that we need more tolerance for deviance, but a recognition that the deviant is providing all of us with a creative opportunity to transcend the limited envelopes in which we wrap ourselves to keep out the cold and thereby make it difficult to continue the metamorphosis of the human species on its evolutionary journey.

Assuming that some consensus has been reached, a lot of possibilities are sometimes rejected because people believe there are no resources to implement them. This is rarely true. A group can, at this point, use a broadening strategy called networking to complement the initial brainstorming.

Networking

Within the constraints of a workshop, networking can be carried out only in a very limited and introductory way. The groups are asked to make lists of all their individual resources, everything they can do, their special interests, talents, hobbies, etc. They then are asked to think of everyone they know who might have resources to offer them (given their special interests, talents, and the plans they have come up with in brainstorming). A certain amount of networking occurs naturally in workshop settings, just as it does at conferences. The following guidelines, we have found, help on a daily basis.

GUIDELINES FOR NETWORKING

1. Have a goal, dream or vision. Examples: making the world interdependent, feeding people, eliminating poverty, ensuring safe neighborhoods.

2. Keep the goal in mind and become fascinated by its possibilities. This gives direction and intentionality to what you are doing.

3. Every contact, every link, is like a new port of entry.

    a. Look in all directions for your resources.

    b. Keep a file on people who want to be helpful. You never know when something will be of use.

    c. Periodically review where you have been and what information you have collected.

4. Give people an opportunity to contribute. Everyone in your network has something of value to share.

5. Contributions people have are the motive force for linking people together. A network is a weaving process. Ask the following question: "How can I best weave these different people together to become valuable resources for one another at this moment?"

6. You are always in a strange land with different customs. Develop a catholic appetite.

7. Check back with people as often as possible with a note or a newsletter.

8. Reminders:

    a. At first your goals may only be of interest to you. However, others can become interested if your goals coincide with theirs.

    b. Listen, keep your eyes open, stay sensitive.

    c. Don't argue with anyone.

    d. Approach each new person and place without expectations. Be ready for anything.

A recent example of our own networking began like a treasure hunt. One day in the Jewish-Christian-Moslem settlement of Neve Shalom in Israel we heard about some wild herbs being grown. A few days later we were visiting with Nuri, a Bedouin chief. He told us about a shortage of doctors among the Bedouin tribes. Because of his knowledge of folk medicine he was called on to administer to his people. We gave Nuri *The Barefoot Doctor's Book*, translated from the Chinese by the U.S. Department of Health, Education, and Welfare. In return, he presented us with a book on herbal and folk medicine, written in Arabic. On the plane to Paris we met a French doctor who taught herbal medicine in Europe who wanted a copy of the herb book. Back in the States we found a publisher who was interested in having the book translated into English for the holistic health network. This led to the idea of a joint business venture to help set up funds for a scholarship for Bedouin children. Subsequently we were introduced to an inventor of a small agricultural machine for growing plants in desert regions with minimal water supplies. Out of this came a design for a water pump. We linked up the inventor with some private investors interested in world hunger and some international development organizations working in villages in Egypt and India. There were many other threads to this story and it still goes on. We sometimes feel like spiders weaving webs that keep growing and interconnecting with other webs.

Our own recent efforts in networking started with a single phone conversation between Denver, Colorado, and Kalamazoo, Michigan, in October 1982. Since that time we have linked up with hundreds of people coast to coast in the United States, and joined with dozens of groups and organizations in Europe, the Middle East, Africa, and Latin America. A resource in one place meets a need in another. Sometimes we discover a resource we don't even know what to do with, and very soon we run across someone who has a use for it. We are not just referring to material resources. Most often the most valuable resources are people themselves with their talents and abilities.

Intentionality and Commitment

Intention or purpose is the impetus behind networking action. It has to do with the goal in mind and the fascination one has with it. To exercise commitment and intentionality, one must understand the relationship between power and responsibility. The existential position that we are totally responsible for all mankind seems awesome, and if people deny their power this sense of responsibility can increase their feelings of guilt and helplessness. The more we discover and develop our power and acknowledge the power of others working with us cooperatively, the less frightening responsibility and commitment appear. Without a recognition of power, choice is an irrelevant concept. What brings power and responsibility together is an increase in awareness — knowing ourselves as well as others — in as many dimensions as possible.

When people enter a state of intentionality and commitment their lives and the lives of those around them are drastically changed. This state is contagious and people with similar goals and aspirations begin to gravitate together and pool their resources. What seemed impossible now becomes possible.

There are many historical examples of this, like General Patton's famous tank drive to rescue the men besieged at Bastogne during World War II. His commitment and intentionality was matched by almost all of the men under his command. A more recent example occurred a few years ago when Shirley McGreal from South Carolina committed herself to rescuing 71,500 monkeys from what she felt was a cruel and unjustified research program run by the U.S. Defense Department. The monkeys were to be exposed to high levels of radiation so that the researchers could study them as they died. The United States government had contracted to buy the monkeys from the government of Bangladesh, which informed Mrs. McGreal that the sale was perfectly legal and that no one in their country really cared about the little "pests" anyway. She flew to Bangladesh and began talking to people in the country about the fate that awaited these monkeys. The people did care about these "pests." They were shocked, and protested in great numbers to their government officials. The officials were surprised because they had not been aware of how strongly their people felt about the monkeys. As a result, the contract to sell the monkeys was cancelled. At this point the American president and his science advisor called in the Bangladeshi ambassador and threatened to cut off some foreign aid if the monkeys weren't delivered. The ambassador informed them that if his government shipped the monkeys there wouldn't be any more need for foreign aid because his government would be out of office. The monkeys stayed home. Shirley McGreal's commitment and intentionality proved to possess more than enough power to take on two large bureaucracies. Shirley McGreal is now head of the International Primate Protection League.

When people are operating at this level they have little time for doomsday scenarios and endless discussions about how difficult it is to get anything done. They also waste little time with those who pay lip service to getting things done. We have no doubt that we can resolve the pressing, dangerous conflicts of our time, as well as successfully find ways to end world hunger. The various solutions are at hand. What is more essential is an appreciation of our own power, the power that becomes manifest only when we enter into a state of commitment and intentionality. When we come in contact with people operating in this way we are usually surprised. We treat them as exceptional or unusual. Yet this exceptional potential is common. The authors have always disliked the term "overachiever," as if it were indeed possible for someone to "overachieve." These people are not over-achieving. They are manifesting the potential they always had. We don't need a great leader or some miraculous new solution. We already have the greatness latent in all of us. Each of us is by our very nature miraculous.

Our intention and commitment can at times become side-tracked, however. This can happen when we become fascinated with some obstacle we encounter on our journey. An all too common example of this comes to mind. Someone leaves the house in the morning to go to work and some other driver "cuts in front" of him. The intention of getting to work is lost as the one cut off begins to focus his energy on the "rude driver" and decides to "teach him a lesson." He may try chasing the other car to write down its license number, or race ahead to cut it off. All too often this leads to a tragic escalation of violence with someone becoming seriously injured. In the process, sight is lost of the larger goal, and a large amount of energy is directed to the "fascinating obstacle." There are hundreds of fascinating obstacles that demand our attention every day. Yet if our focus is clearly on our goal and we keep firmly yet lovingly to our intentions, the obstacles can be easily overcome with a minimum expenditure of energy.

When one of the authors was in graduate school he lived with a large group of students in a big house, and often studied in the living room. Roommates came in and out of the room talking. Initially they would stop to ask questions such as "Who's home?" "When's dinner?" and "Did so and so call?" When he was studying he rarely responded or even heard what was asked. Soon they stopped talking to him at these times. He never asked anyone to leave him alone. They came to respect his commitment to his work. Sometimes they would kid him at supper about his "deafness." People who could have been "obstacles" became a helpful support group and often brought him coffee without his asking or performing some other courtesy that made his work easier.

A couple of years ago the same author was with a group of six people in a special training program at the Esalen Institute in California. Their guide and instructor was George Leonard. They were studying Leonard Energy Training and aikido. Esalen is a very relaxed place, yet the six of them were participating in a rigorous and intense program that lasted for two months. They worked from 6:00 A.M. to midnight. In the morning they worked in silence until 9:30 A.M. They had taken voluntary vows of silence. At first, the rest of the Esalen community was somewhat skeptical of this group and what they were doing. This soon changed to respect and then active support. After the third week the world around them subtly began to change. They would be in the food line in the morning for breakfast and some new person would come up to them and start to talk. A resident of the community who they hardly knew would intervene and tell the new person that they weren't allowed to talk in the morning. Their own loving dedication and commitment gradually transformed the atmosphere around them. Obstacles melted away and people became willing, active supporters of what they were doing. They never asked anyone else to change what they were doing or tried to get them to accommodate their behavior to their way of being. They created and lived in an energy field that became infectious to those around them. It was impressive and humbling to be a part of such a beautiful process.

We would like to contrast this to an approach our government has pursued for many years. It's called MAD, Mutually Assured Destruction, and it means being willing to meet obstacles head-on as in the diagram on the following page.

If we are committed to life and not MAD, it is possible and even probable to increase the likelihood of our grandchildren remembering us. We don't believe in pie in the sky or the idea that if we suffer enough on earth we will be rewarded in heaven. Like William James, we invite you to live your life with us "as if we can make a difference" in this world, not in the next. For it is in this world, right now, where spiritual values can be brought into existence through love, disciplined work, and commitment to creating a supportive environment for all of the world's people.

THE MAD (Mutually Assured Destruction) BOOM SOLUTION

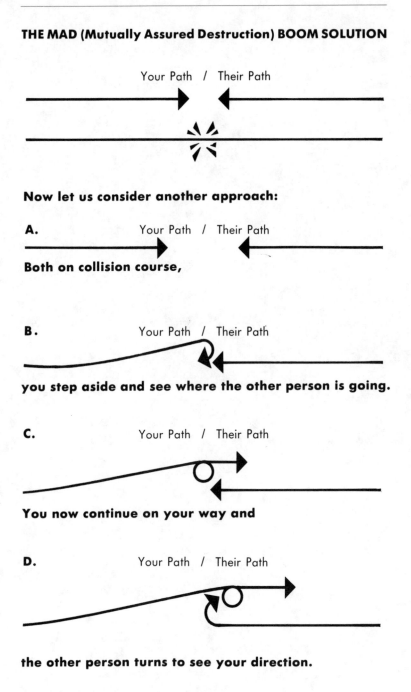

Now let us consider another approach:

A.   Your Path / Their Path

Both on collision course,

B.   Your Path / Their Path

you step aside and see where the other person is going.

C.   Your Path / Their Path

You now continue on your way and

D.   Your Path / Their Path

the other person turns to see your direction.

EPILOGUE

The challenge of our time is in the opportunity either to resist or accept change and conflict. If we fight and resist conflict we learn little from it and prevent ourselves from arriving at a more fulfilling resolution. We can learn to see conflict as a natural part of the process of nature.

It is especially incumbent upon us to release ourselves from resistance now, at a time when we have become so differentiated and powerful as individuals. Can we still love and connect with others and with the whole to gain a sense of interdependence and responsibility, or will we destroy ourselves by remaining in the split between self and other, and self and nature, by resisting unity?

For the first time in our history we have the power to rupture the connections for other nations and for ourselves. If we continue to deny the new balance that seeks to come into existence, conflict will worsen and our power may become uncontrollable. In this denial we generate a growing mistrust and we could unleash the violent weapons we have accumulated to destroy the external sources of our frustration, the "enemy," as well as ourselves. This kind of violent purging is an absurd solution to the challenge of conflict.

Let's imagine a world where both at home and in school children are taught that each person is special and unique, and that through cooperative behavior they can get their needs met. We imagine a world where family disputes are handled within the family, where communities work to maximize the creative potential of every person, where universities are dedicated to exploring new frontiers as well as passing on the wisdom of the ages, and where artists and musicians join with other citizens to celebrate the joy, tragedy, and mystery of life. We imagine a world where people feel so comfortable with themselves and their needs that they create a multitude of ways of meeting them, a world where each creature is part of an evolving dance of excellence.

A Visit to a Museum in the Year 2084

Daughter: "What's that, Mommy?"
Mother: "Oh, that's a statue of a policeman."
Son: "What's a policeman?"
Father: "He used to protect people against crime."
Children: "What's crime?"
Mother: "Well, it's something that used to happen when people hadn't learned how to get their needs met."
Children: "Oh. Can we go look at the dinosaur now?"

We invite the readers of this book to write to us of their hopes and aspirations, of those times when they experienced a heightened awareness, a sense of transformation, and of moments they felt that glorious feeling of purpose and hope for all of us on this small precious gem in the cosmos we call earth.

SUGGESTED READINGS

Arms, Suzanne. *Immaculate Deception: A New Look at Women and Childbirth in America*. New York: Houghton Mifflin, 1975.

Bateson, Gregory. *"Crisis in the Mind,"* Part 4 in *Steps to an Ecology of Mind*. New York: Ballantine, 1972.

Boulding, Kenneth. "What Teach-Ins Taught Us." *Dissent* 13 (January-February 1966): 10.

Dobson, Terry. *Giving in to Get Your Way*. New York: Delacorte, 1978.

Ferguson, Marilyn. *The Aquarian Conspiracy*. Los Angeles: Jeremy P. Tarcher, 1981.

Fisher, Roger, and Ury, William. *Getting to Yes, Negotiating Without Giving In*. New York: Penguin, 1983.

Grefe, Edward A. *Fighting to Win*. New York: Harcort Brace Jovanovich, 1981.

Hare, Paul A. "Small Group Discussions with Participatory and Supervisory Leadership." *Journal of Abnormal and Social Psychology* 48 (1953): 273.

Jordan, Brigette. *Birth in Four Cultures: Cross-Cultural Investigation of Childbirth in the Yucatan, Holland, Sweden and the United States*. Toronto: Eden Press, 1980.

Knapp, Mark L. *Interpersonal Communication and Human Relationships*. Newton, Mass.: Allyn and Bacon, 1984.

Kramer, Joel. *The Passionate Mind*. Milibrae, Calif.: Celestial Arts, 1974.

Lacey, Robert. *The Kingdom: Arabia and The House of Sa'ud*. New York: Avon, 1981.

Leonard, George. *The Silent Pulse*. New York: E. P. Dutton, 1978.

Miller, Wackman, Nunnally, and Saline. *Straight Talk*. New York: New American Library, 1981.

Naisbitt, John. *Megatrends*. New York: Warner Books, 1982.

Nixon, Richard. *Leaders*. New York: Warner Books, 1982.

Peters, Thomas, and Waterman, Robert. *In Search of Excellence*. New York: Warner Books, 1984.

Raiffa, Howard. *The Art and Science of Navigation*. Cambridge: Harvard University Press, 1982.

Putney, Snell and Gail. *The Adjusted American*. New York: Harper & Row, 1964.

Robertson, Dougal. *Survive the Savage Sea*. New York: Praeger, 1973.

Sanders, Marion *The Professional Radical: Conversations with Saul Alinsky*. New York: Harper & Row, 1970.

Sherif, Muzafer.. "Experiments in Group Conflict." *Scientific American* 195 (November 1956): 54.

Sullivan, Harry Stack. *The Collected Works of Harry Stack Sullivan*. Vol. 2. New York: W. W. Norton & Co., 1964.

Thomas, Lewis. "An Argument for Cooperation." *Discover* 5 (August 1984): 66.

Tarkenton, Fran. *Playing to Win: Strategies for Business Success*. New York: Harper & Row, 1982.

Villado, Alberto, and Dychtwald, Kenneth. *Millenium: Glimpses into the 21st Century*. Los Angeles: Jeremy P. Tarcher, 1981.

Wedge, Bryant. "A Psychiatric Model for Intercession in Group Conflict." *Journal of Applied Behaviorial Science* 6 (October-November-December 1971): 494

Zinker, Joseph. *Creative Process in Gestalt Therapy*. New York: Vintage Books, 1981.